GOLF FORE!! BEGINNERS

THE FUNDAMENTALS

by STEPHEN J. RUTHENBERG

RGS PUBLISHING
Lansing, Michigan

*Additional copies of this book may be ordered through bookstores
or by sending $9.95 plus $2.75 for postage and handling to:*
Publishers Distribution Service
121 E. Front Street, Suite 203
Traverse City, MI 49684
1-800-345-0096

Front cover and Photographs by Gary Schrewberry
Illustrations by Denny Arnett

Publisher's Cataloging-in-Publication Data

Ruthenberg, Stephen J., 1961-
  Golf "fore" beginners : the FUNdamentals / by
Stephen J. Ruthenberg.--Lansing, Michigan :
RGS Publishing.
    p.   ill.   cm.
  ISBN 0-9631514-1-X
  1. Golf.   I. Title.   II. Title: Golf fore beginners.
III. Title: Golf for beginners.

GV965.R88   1992
796.352--dc20   91-67566

First Edition

10 9 8 7 6 5 4 3 2 1

Manufactured in the United States of America

*To my wife, Karen, for all her support
and input throughout the project,
for only she can truly appreciate the
magnitude of developing this book.*

To our children, Jason and Amy Lynn.

To my parents for their commitment to their children.

For my mother - may God bless her soul.

ACKNOWLEDGMENTS

This book would not be possible without the efforts and help of a number of people. Thanks are due to: a long-time friend, Paul Gilmet, whose concern for golfers and the welfare of the game of golf led to the production of this book; Bruce Fossum for introducing me to Publishers Distribution Service; to Alex Moore of Publishers Distribution Service for putting the book together. Thanks also to: photographer Gary Schrewberry and those who made the cover possible; Mike Spencer for modeling in the photographs; Denny Arnett for developing the many illustrations to help make the book easy to understand. The title is the brainchild of Keith Warriner. Also, thanks to those who edited the book to assure accuracy.

Fortunately, I have worked with some of the finest golf professionals in the country. I appreciate their assistance in helping me to grow professionally. Most of all, a special thanks to John Schlaman, a lifelong friend and fellow golf professional. I would not be in the golf business today without John's help - thanks Schlaa.

CONTENTS

ABOUT THE AUTHOR

Stephen Ruthenberg has over 12 years of experience in the golf business, and has been an active member of the Professional Golfers' Association of America for more than five years. Throughout his 12 years in the business, he has instructed numerous golf classes along with hundreds of individual golf lessons. Currently, he is employed as the Head Golf Professional at Michigan State University's Forest Akers Golf Courses. Steve is a 1984 graduate of Ferris State University, in Big Rapids Michigan, with a bachelor's degree in Marketing/Professional Golf Management.

Throughout his career, he has been actively involved in promoting the game of golf. As a result, in 1991, the golf operation at Michigan State University received the National Golf Foundation's Public Achievement Award for their contributions to promoting golf in America.

INTRODUCTION

The goal of this book is to provide you with a simple and informative introduction to the game of golf. Regardless of your age or gender, if you are a beginner or have limited golf experience, *Golf Fore!! Beginners* provides a complete guide to learning the game of golf. If you feel intimidated or apprehensive about the game, this book will eliminate any such feelings and introduce the game so it is easy to understand and fun to learn. Over 100 illustrations and photographs are included throughout the text to assure each topic is easily understood.

Chapters 1 through 5 of the book introduce you to the game and answer your questions about the layout of a golf course, score keeping, equipment, golf etiquette, and rules for the game of golf. Chapters 6 through 8 highlight how to set up for a golf swing by reviewing the grip, body posture, ball position, and alignment. In Chapters 9 through 11, you will learn how to execute different shots used in golf including the full swing with your woods and irons, putting, chipping, pitching, half to three-quarter shots, and bunker shots. Chapters 12 through 15 provide helpful hints for practicing and playing the game, and a guide to purchasing your golf equipment. Last, there is a complete glossary of golf related terms.

To simplify the instruction, the text is written for a right-handed golfer. If you are a left-handed golfer, please reverse the terms when the text refers to your left or right.

GOLF FORE!! BEGINNERS

THE FUNDAMENTALS

1

WELCOME TO
THE GAME OF GOLF

HISTORY

As early as the 15th century, a game similar to golf was played in Scotland with a club made of a bent tree branch and a small leather bag stuffed with feathers for a ball. The game as we know it today originated in St. Andrews, Scotland in 1744. The first official golf course in America was built in 1888 in Yonkers, New York, called "The St. Andrews Golf Club." The course originally had three holes, then expanded to six holes, nine holes and finally eighteen holes.

Golf continued to grow in popularity in America. However, by the turn of the century, the game was played primarily by wealthy people who had time and money to dedicate to the game. In 1913, a 20-year-old caddie, Francis Ouimet, stunned the nation when he became the first American to win the U.S. Open at "The Country Club," in his hometown of Brookline, Massachusetts. From that day on, the game of golf has become increasingly popular in America. Today, there are over 24 million golfers in the United States.

GOLF - THE GAME OF A LIFETIME

Golf is the most widely played game in the world. Whether you are male or female, and regardless of your age, you can enjoy the great game of golf. Children play with adults, men and women play together, and all may enjoy the game equally. Unlike many other sports, you do not need special athletic ability to enjoy the game.

Golf offers a wide variety of benefits. The game is played outside on some of the most beautiful pieces of land throughout the world. Golf can be a form of exercise. Walking 18 holes is equivalent to walking 5 miles. The game is a great family activity, for children, parents and grandparents. Businesses throughout the world use the game to promote their companies. Organizations use golf outings to raise money for charities. Some regions use golf as a major attraction for their tourism, providing millions or even billions of dollars to their economy.

Many people use golf for relaxation, to get away from their everyday pressures and to enjoy the atmosphere the game offers. The game builds relationships with friends, family and business associates. Golf teaches you to deal with adversity. To excel at the game, you will learn discipline, dedication and patience. But most of all, *the game is fun!*

OBJECT OF THE GAME

The game of golf is played outdoors, on an area of land that is referred to as a *golf course*. Each course normally consists of *9* or *18 holes*. When you play 9 or 18 holes, you are playing a *round* of golf.

The object of each hole is to hit the golf ball into a *cup*. The starting point of each hole is the *teeing ground*. The finishing point is the cup, located on the *putting green*. Any attempt to hit the golf ball, whether successful or unsuccessful is considered a *stroke*. When playing, *golf clubs* are used to hit the golf ball. These clubs vary in length and design, and are referred to as *woods, irons,* or *putters. The object of the game is to play all 9 or 18 holes, taking*

*as few strokes as possible to get your ball from the teeing
ground into the cup on each hole.*

DETERMINING YOUR SCORE

Every hole on a golf course is assigned a *par* of either
three, four, or *five.* The par is based on the length of the
hole which is measured in *yards.* As shown in figure 1.1,
the guideline used to determine par is different for men
and women.

PAR	WOMEN	PAR	MEN
3	up to 210 yards	3	up to 250 yards
4	211-400	4	251-470
5	401-575	5	471 and over

[Figure 1.1]
Determining Par

Par is the number of strokes in which you try to
complete each hole. It is a mark of excellence for playing
the hole. When playing the game, you compare your
strokes with par. Only the finest golfers play golf at or
below par. When you first start playing, do not expect to
score near par. For instance, on a par-4, it may be common for you to take eight to ten strokes.

On a par-3, your goal is to get from the tee onto the
putting green in one stroke. On a par-4, your goal is two
strokes, and on a par-5, your goal is three strokes. Once
on the green your goal is to putt the ball into the hole in
two strokes or less.

KEEPING SCORE-THE SCORECARD

Hole Layout

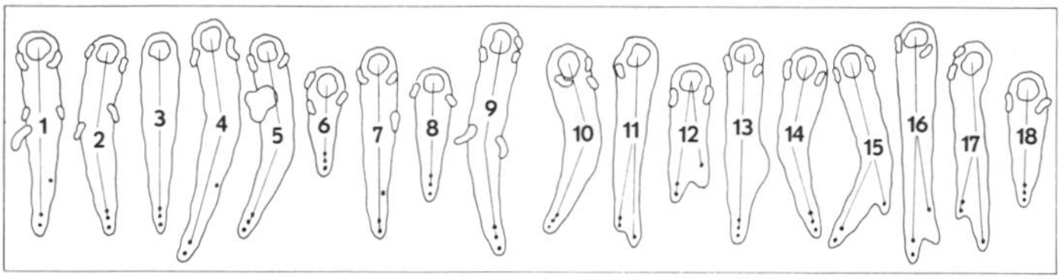

Length of Hole

Men's Par

Women's Par

Holes	1	2	3	4	5	6	7	8	9	Out	10	11	12	13	14	15	16	17	18	In	Tot	Hcp	Net
Blue	419	380	416	525	410	181	385	237	474	3427	339	441	201	390	334	435	590	394	199	3323	6750		
White	405	369	408	480	394	173	363	218	462	3272	332	395	188	377	316	402	577	353	188	3128	6400		
Handicap	5	13	7	15	3	9	11	1	17		18	2	8	6	14	4	16	12	10				
Par	4	4	4	5	4	3	4	3	5	36	4	4	3	4	4	4	5	4	3	35	71		
+ / —																							
Par	4	4	4	5	4	3	4	3	5	36	4	4	3	4	4	4	5	4	3	35	71		
Red	318	358	400	369	325	165	314	199	449	2897	325	386	114	364	299	322	465	343	177	2795	5692		
Handicap	1	11	9	3	7	15	17	5	13		18	4	12	10	16	8	2	14	6				

(PLAYER)

Date ___ Scorer ___ Attest ___

COURSE RATINGS: Blue 72.5 White 71.0 Red 72.9
SLOPE 123 119 121

[Figure 1.2]
Scorecard
(Scorecard Courtesy of Golf Associates Scorecard Company, Asheville, NC)

Your ability as a golfer is determined by the number of strokes it takes you to play each hole. When starting the game, do not focus too much attention on your score. Simply get used to playing the game and being on the golf course.

Regardless of whether you keep score or not, always get a *scorecard* from the golf shop before starting your round of golf. Figure 1.2. The scorecard is a helpful aid. First, scorecards show the length and par of each hole. Second, they often show a drawing or layout of each hole identifying the location of rivers, ponds, bunkers, etc. Third, if you are playing in a competition using *handicaps,* the handicap to be used for each hole is shown on the scorecard (handicapping will be discussed later in this chapter).

When looking at the scorecard, people often ask what the terms *out* and *in* mean. *Out* is where you put your total score for the first nine holes. *In* is where you put your total score for the second nine holes. This assumes you started on hole number one. The terms originated with the links style courses in Scotland that follow the seaside or bay. It is common for the first nine holes to go out away from the clubhouse, along the shoreline. The second nine holes are adjacent to the first nine, but go back in toward the clubhouse.

SCORING TERMS

The following are terms commonly used to refer to your score on each hole. An *ace* or *hole-in-one* refers to getting your ball in the hole in one stroke and is extremely rare. Also rare is a *double eagle* which is three strokes under par. An *eagle* is two under par, while a *birdie* is one under par. It is more common to have scores over par. For instance, a *bogey* is one over par, a *double bogey* is two over par, a *triple bogey* is three over par, and a *quadruple bogey* is four over par.

HANDICAP

A *handicap* is a number assigned to a golfer, based on the scores he or she normally shoots. Handicaps are used so golfers of different abilities can compete against each other. A person is not required to have a handicap in order to play golf, however, some golf tournaments require that you have an established handicap to participate. If you become interested in obtaining a handicap it is best to contact a local golf course that has a handicap service.

2

THE LAYOUT OF
THE GOLF COURSE

Many sports are played in a standard setting regardless of where they are played. For instance, basketball, tennis, and football are all played on a standardized setting. Regardless of what court or field you play on, the size and dimensions are always the same. Golf, however, is played on courses that vary due to their natural surroundings. Golf courses are built over large parcels of land, so with every parcel of land comes a different setting. There are numerous golf courses throughout the world, with every hole on each course varying in length, design, and character. In addition, courses themselves are always changing as the weather, and seasons have their impact. Figure 2.1 illustrates the layout of a golf hole.

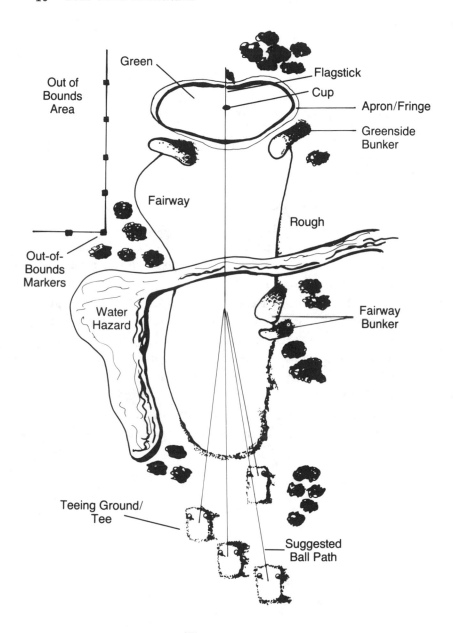

[Figure 2.1]
Layout of a Golf Hole

THE TEEING GROUND

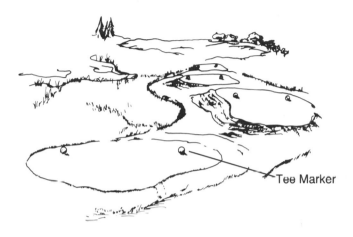

[Figure 2.2]
Teeing Ground

The starting point for each hole is called the *teeing ground* or *tee*. Figure 2.2. The term tee also refers to a small wooden tool used to elevate the golf ball off the ground when attempting to play your first stroke from the teeing ground. Located on the teeing ground are tee markers which are set apart to designate the starting point for the hole. Originally, golf courses only had one set of tee markers. More tee markers have been added to challenge men and women with different abilities. Today, some of the newer courses have between four and five sets of tees, offering maximum flexibility for the golfer. You will see three sets of tee markers at most courses you play. These markers are color coordinated, and the colors may vary at different courses. Normally, the front tee markers, or the ones closest to the green, are red. The middle tee markers are white and the back tee markers blue.

Traditionally, the red tee markers are the ladies' regular tees. The white tees are the men's regular tees, or ladies' championship tees. And the blue tees are the men's championship tees. As a beginning golfer, use the regular tee markers.

THE FAIRWAY

[Figure 2.3]
The Fairway

When starting each hole, the object is to hit the ball from the tee onto the *fairway,* sometimes referred to as the short grass. Figure 2.3. Normally there are advantages to hitting the ball onto the fairway. First, the grass in the fairway is closely mowed and well-maintained, which makes it easier to hit your next shot. Second, there are fewer obstacles such as water hazards, bunkers, trees, bushes, or mounds for your ball to hit or land in. Third, the fairway often offers the shortest route to the hole. A shot that is hit poorly and lands in the fairway is often better than a shot hit well that curves into the rough.

THE ROUGH

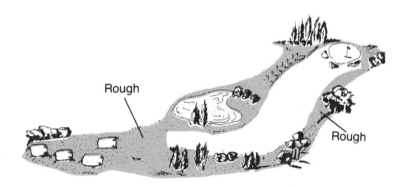

Rough

Rough

[Figure 2.4]
The Rough

The *rough* is generally considered a less desirable area for your ball to land. Figure 2.4. It is the area bordering the fairway, teeing ground and putting green. This area is called the "rough" because it is often more difficult to hit your ball from the rough than it is to hit your ball from the fairway. The grass in the rough is usually longer than the grass in the fairway.

The rough also offers other difficulties, such as water hazards, bunkers, trees, bushes or mounds which may affect your swing or the flight of your golf ball. Each course is different. Some keep the grass in the rough long, while others keep the rough short.

WATER HAZARDS

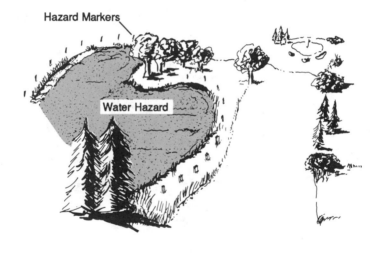

[Figure 2.5]
Water Hazard

Golf courses may have water in or along many locations of the course in the form of oceans, seas, lakes, ponds, rivers, creeks, or marshes. These areas are referred to as *water hazards*, and are areas in which you do not want to hit your golf ball. Figure 2.5. As a beginner, having to hit over water may be intimidating and frustrating. However, as you play the game more, you will find that these hazards test your ability as a golfer and add enjoyment to the game. Water hazards are marked with *red* or *yellow stakes* or *lines*.

Water hazards also serve other important purposes for the golf course. Architects often use water hazards to enhance the beauty of a golf course. In addition, with the demand for water increasing in many regions throughout the world, it is important for golf courses to have a large supply of fresh water to maintain the turf and reduce maintenance costs.

If you elect, you may play a shot from within a water hazard. If this is not possible, the rules discussed in Chapter 5 explain your various options.

BUNKERS

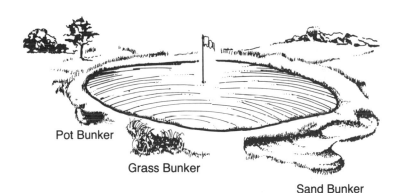

Pot Bunker

Grass Bunker

Sand Bunker

[Figure 2.6]
Types of Bunkers

When designing a golf course, the architect often will put *bunkers* in strategic locations on each hole to test the skill of the golfer. It is best to keep your ball out of the bunkers, because they can be difficult to hit out of. Bunkers are considered a hazard, like water hazards. Bunkers normally have a sand base and are referred to as a sand trap. Figure 2.6. However, the proper name is bunker. Bunkers with a grass base are called *grass bunkers*. When bunkers are placed in the fairway, they are referred to as *fairway bunkers,* and *greenside bunkers* are near the green. Like water hazards, bunkers are also used to improve the scenery of a golf hole. When properly designed, an architect can make a flat, unattractive parcel of land look very pleasing with bunkers.

OUT-OF-BOUNDS

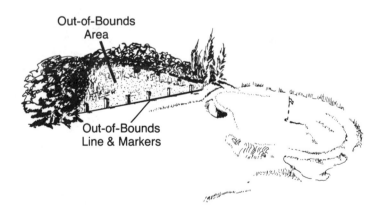

[Figure 2.7]
Out-of-Bounds

Every course has boundaries. *Out-of-bounds* is the area in which play is prohibited. When playing golf you will notice the area of the course that is out-of-bounds, because it will be marked with *white posts* or a *continuous white line*. Figure 2.7. The scorecard also indicates the out-of-bounds areas. If you find your ball in an area marked out-of-bounds, you cannot play your next shot from there. A shot hit out-of-bounds must be replayed from the spot where it was last hit.

THE GREEN

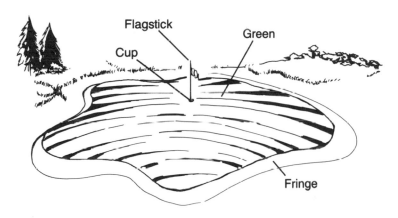

[Figure 2.8]
The Green

The *putting green,* or *green,* is an immaculately-maintained grass surface where the hole, or *cup,* is located. Figure 2.8. The green is specially designed to include mounding, contouring and sloping to add challenge to the shots around the green. The green is the most expensive part of the course to build and maintain. The grass is of a special type which needs to be mowed and watered daily.

The hole is 4 1/4 inches in diameter. It is normally moved to a different location on the green each morning, to reduce traffic wear on the green. A *flagstick,* which is a long straight pole with a flag on top, is used to identify the location of the cup on the green. Many courses have a *plastic ball* or an additional *smaller flag* located on the flagstick to inform you whether the cup is located on the front, middle or back portion of the green. Figure 2.9.

Located around the green is a slightly higher level of grass called the *fringe,* or *apron.* Figure 2.8. This area is not as smooth or closely-mowed as the putting green.

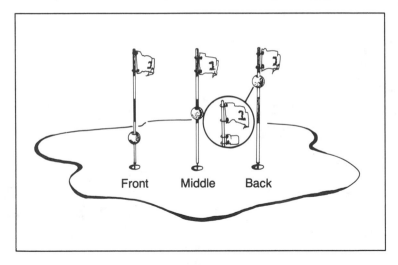

[Figure 2.9]
Hole Location

GOLF'S UNIT OF MEASUREMENT - THE YARD

Any time you refer to distance on the golf course, it is stated in *yards.* For instance, the length of each hole, the distance you hit each shot, the range each club will hit the ball, and the distance from your ball to the green are all measured in yards. Yardage guides often are available in a variety of forms at golf courses. To help golfers determine the distance they need to hit each shot, some courses offer *yardage booklets* that list specific landmarks and their distances to other points on the hole. Many courses also put *yardage markers* in the center or side of the fairway to inform golfers of the yardage to the green. The most common marker is the 150 yard marker, with 100 and 200 yard markers also used. Some courses put the distance from the sprinkler heads to the green on the sprinkler head. Other courses use selected landmarks like trees, or bunkers to determine the distance to the green. Always check to see if the measurements are made to the center of the green or front of the green, because this can make a difference in how far you need your shot to go.

3

YOUR GOLF CLUBS

To maximize your enjoyment of golf, it is important to have an understanding about the equipment. First, the game is played with a set of golf clubs which include *woods, irons,* and a *putter.* A complete set of clubs is composed of a maximum of 14 clubs. You may mix the number of woods and irons in any combination you like. Most golfers have eight to eleven irons, two to five woods and a putter. Figure 3.1 shows a normal set of golf clubs with the exception of a putter.

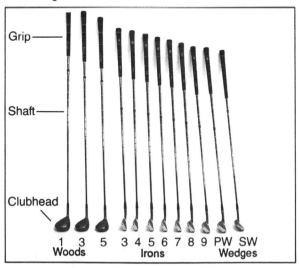

[Figure 3.1]
Irons and Woods

CLUB CHARACTERISTICS

Both woods and irons vary in *length* and *loft*. The difference in the length of the clubs is shown in figure 3.1. The loft refers to the angle of the *clubface*. Figure 3.2. The loft for each club varies, as shown in figures 3.3 and 3.4. Together, the length and loft of a club affect the distance and height of a shot, also referred to as the *trajectory*. Figure 3.5.

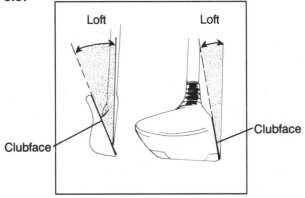

[Figure 3.2]
Loft of a Wood and Iron

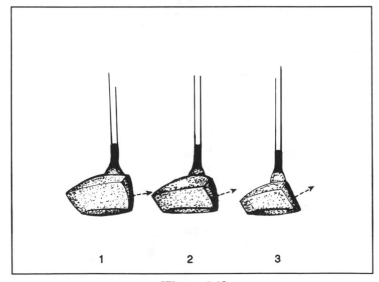

[Figure 3.3]
Loft of Various Woods

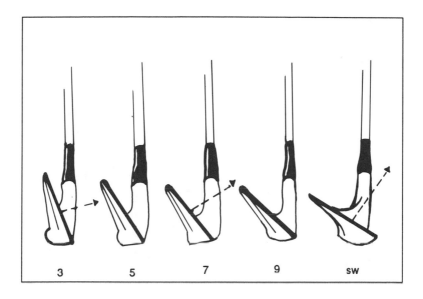

[Figure 3.4]
Loft of Various Irons

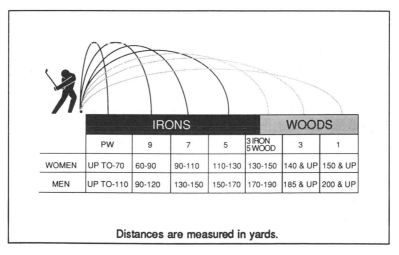

	IRONS					WOODS	
	PW	9	7	5	3 IRON 5 WOOD	3	1
WOMEN	UP TO-70	60-90	90-110	110-130	130-150	140 & UP	150 & UP
MEN	UP TO-110	90-120	130-150	150-170	170-190	185 & UP	200 & UP

Distances are measured in yards.

[Figure 3.5]
Trajectory & Range of Distance for Average Golfers

WOODS

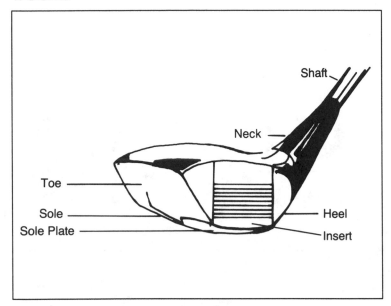

[Figure 3.6]
Wood

Figure 3.6 shows the clubhead of a *wood* and the terms associated with it. Woods are designed to hit the ball farther than irons. They range from a 1-wood to a 14-wood. Normally, your woods will be between the numbers 1 and 5, with other numbers very rare. Today, when purchasing a set of woods, the most common combination includes the 1-, 3- and the 5-wood. The 4-wood is still fairly popular, while the 2-wood is seldom manufactured anymore.

Woods vary in length, with the 1-wood, also called the *driver,* being the longest club manufactured. Each club decreases in length by a half inch as the number of the club increases. For instance, if a 1-wood is 43 inches in length, a 3-wood would be 42 inches, and a 5-wood 41 inches.

While the 1-wood is referred to as the driver, all other woods are called *fairway woods*. Normally, the driver is used only from the teeing ground because the clubhead is larger, which makes it difficult to hit the ball if it is not on a tee. All other woods are most commonly used from the fairway, or rough, when the distance from the ball to the green is too great to reach by using an iron. As shown in figure 3.3, fairway woods are designed with a smaller clubhead and more loft, which makes the club easier to use from the fairway or rough.

As a beginner, it is quite common to experience more difficulty using the driver than the other clubs because the driver is longer than other clubs, the clubface has less loft, and the clubhead is larger. Therefore, if you are having trouble hitting your driver from the teeing ground, you may start by using a 3-wood or 5-wood.

IRONS

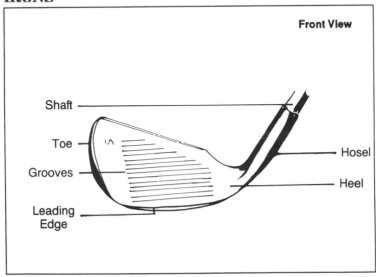

[Figure 3.7]
Iron

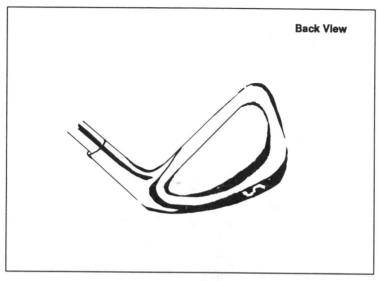

[Figure 3.7]
Iron

As you get closer to the green, you use clubs called *irons*. Figure 3.7 shows the clubhead of an iron from the front and back, along with the terms associated with it. Like woods, irons are identified by their number and vary in one-half inch increments. Irons range from 1 through 9, plus the wedges. The longest iron is the 1-iron and the shortest irons are the wedges. The closer you are to the green, the higher number iron you will use. Generally, a set of irons consist of the 3-iron through the 9-iron and a pitching wedge. For the more experienced golfer, a 1- and 2-iron may also be included in a set.

WEDGES

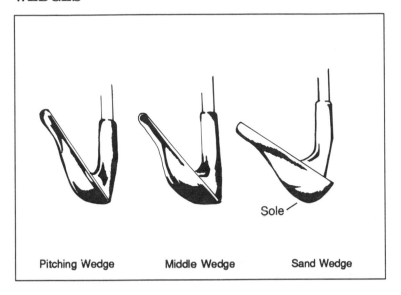

[Figure 3.8]
Types of Wedges

Wedges are also considered irons. They are designed
to hit the ball high and short, and are used for a variety
of shots around the green. Originally, the game was played
with only one wedge, the pitching wedge. As the game of
golf changes, so does the equipment. Today there are three
wedges available for your set: *the pitching wedge, middle
wedge, and sand wedge.* Figure 3.8. All golfers should use
at least two wedges, the pitching wedge and the sand
wedge. The sand wedge is not usually included when
purchasing a set of irons, but you should definitely include
a sand wedge for your set, because it is one of the most
frequently-used clubs. The *sole,* or bottom, of the sand
wedge is larger than other wedges, which helps get the
ball out of the sand. The sand wedge also has more loft

than other irons, and may help when playing shots from the grass near the green.

An optional wedge for your set of clubs is the middle wedge. In recent years, the middle wedge has been introduced, offering more loft than the pitching wedge. This allows shots near the green to fly higher and roll less. Furthermore, this wedge has a smaller sole than the sand wedge, to make it easier to hit the ball from the grass.

PUTTERS

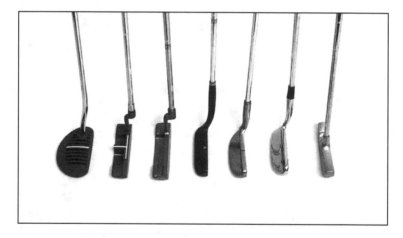

[Figure 3.9]
Various Putters

Putters are designed to be used on or near the putting green. The club is designed to roll the golf ball, not loft the ball in the air. As shown in figure 3.9, there are a wide variety of putters in many different lengths and designs.

MAINTENANCE OF YOUR GOLF CLUBS

Generally speaking, golf equipment is designed to be quite durable and maintenance-free. Annually, you should check your *grips* to make sure they are in good condition. Depending on how often you play, your grips will last three months to two years. When necessary, a golf professional or club-fitter can change your grips.

Headcovers are suggested to protect your woods. If you have woods with a graphite or boron shaft, your headcovers should be long enough to protect the shaft also. Covers are also available for your irons, but these are not necessary. Your irons are designed to be durable, and the covers will not provide much additional protection.

4

GOLF ETIQUETTE

Like other games, sports or activities, the game of golf has specific etiquette and rules that should be followed. The term etiquette means recommended conduct, or polite behavior. For years the game of golf has been known as a gentlemen's game, referring to the fact that all golfers should respect the golf course and their fellow golfers. As you continue to play the game, you will appreciate others using proper etiquette. As a beginner, you may be nervous or worried about what to do or not do on the golf course. To help eliminate this uncertainty, *this chapter will answer most of your questions about golf course behavior.*

PROPER ETIQUETTE ON THE PUTTING GREEN

The *green* is the most expensive part of the course to build and maintain. Therefore, special care should be taken to assure the playing surface of the green is kept as nice as possible.

Fixing Your Ball Mark

[Figure 4.1]
Fixing A Ball Mark

When the ball lands on the green, it often leaves a mark or dent in the green. This mark should be fixed with a *ball mark repair tool* or a tee. Figure 4.1. A *ball mark* fixed immediately heals within 24 hours. A ball mark that is not fixed immediately takes 30 days to heal. A good rule of thumb to follow is; always fix your ball mark plus one additional ball mark on each green. Tools are available in most golf shops for a nominal fee.

Tending The Flagstick

If it is difficult to see the hole when putting, you may have the flagstick held, also called *tended,* while you putt. The person tending the flagstick should hold the flag against the flagstick so that it does not rattle in the wind. Also, do not stand on anyone's line or have your shadow over the line of the person putting. After the person has hit their putt, the person tending the flag should take the flagstick out of the cup immediately, so that the ball does not hit the flagstick as it enters the cup.

The Flagstick

When handling the flagstick, make sure that it does not dent the green. When setting the flagstick down, lay it down carefully. Do not drop or throw it. Also, make sure that the flagstick is placed away from the hole so that it will not interfere with anyone's putt.

Footwear For The Green

Make sure the shoes you are wearing will not damage the putting green. Golf shoes or tennis shoes are recommended, but double-check the sole because some golf and tennis shoes can damage the green. Check with a golf professional or reputable golf retailer to help select the correct footwear. When using golf shoes with spikes, pick up your feet while walking so you do not leave excessive spike marks.

Where To Put Your Equipment

Never bring your golf bag, pull cart, or power cart onto the putting green. Leave them on the side of the green closest to the next tee.

Do's And Don'ts On The Putting Green:

Do's...

1. Always mark your ball on the green with a ball marker before others putt. Figure 4.2.

2. After marking your ball, if your ball marker is in the line of another player's putt, then move your mark over one or two putter head lengths.

3. Always take your ball out of the hole immediately after you make your putt.

[Figure 4.2]
Marking A Ball

Don't...
1. Step on the hole; walk around it.

2. Stand too close to the hole when a fellow golfer is putting.

3. Step on the line or path from the ball to the hole of another player's putt.

4. Let your shadow fall over the line or path of another player's putt.

5. Stand along the line of another player's putt, so they can see you while they are putting.

THROUGHOUT THE COURSE

When To Hit

Make sure each golfer in the previous group is out of range before hitting your next shot. When in doubt, you are better off to wait.

Order of Play

The player whose ball is farthest from the hole should hit first. Two players should not hit at the same time. The order of play to start each hole is determined from the score on the previous hole. The person with the lowest score on the previous hole should play first. If there is a tie on the previous hole, then the last person to have had the lowest score would go first. The person with the lowest score on the previous hole is said to have the *honor* on the teeing ground.

[Figure 4.3]
Equipment Placement and Where To Stand

Where To Put Your Equipment When Playing

Your bag, pull cart, or power cart should always be placed where they will not interfere with your swing, as shown in figure 4.3. Do not place your equipment behind you, so you do not trip on it. Also, never bring your golf bag, pull cart, or power cart onto the teeing ground, green, or into the bunker.

Where To Stand When Other Players Are Hitting

Figure 4.3 also shows the correct spot to stand when other players are hitting. For safety purposes, do not stand ahead of anyone while they are hitting the ball.

The Word "Fore"

Always yell the word *fore,* if your shot inadvertently goes toward other golfers. Shout loudly and early enough so they have time to react. If you hear the word fore, *do not look up.* Turn your face and chest away from the direction of the warning, lean toward the ground and cover your head.

Replace All Your Divots

[Figure 4.4]
A Divot

When hitting the ball, it is common to take grass, called a *divot,* as shown in figure 4.4. Remember to take a few seconds after your shot to replace your divot. A divot replaced immediately will grow back to normal within one week. A hole left from a divot can take up to six months to grow back to normal.

Rake The Bunker When Leaving

After you hit your shot out of the *bunker,* rake the sand to eliminate your footprints and club marks. If your ball lands in a footprint in the bunker, you must play the ball from that location.

Playing Through

Playing through means that you let the group of golfers behind you play the remaining holes ahead of you. It is common courtesy to let faster golfers play through. When letting players through, make sure that you are not in the way, and are protected from a possible errant shot.

Follow All Power Golf Cart Rules

Always follow the cart rules at the course. If no rules are posted, keep the cart 50 feet from all greens and tees unless you are on a cart path.

Lightning

For safety purposes, never play golf when there is lightning. If you are on the course and you see lightning, immediately mark the location of your ball, and seek shelter. If possible, it is best to get back to the clubhouse. Some courses also have shelters on the course. Never use a tree for shelter, because trees attract lightning.

SPEED OF PLAY

The number one problem with golf today is the time it takes to play a round of golf. Many golfers would like to play more often, but cannot due to the time it takes to complete a round. With a *foursome,* which is a group of four golfers, 9 holes should be completed in a maximum two hours, and 18 holes in a maximum four hours. At some courses, when playing at peak times, it can take up to three hours to play 9 holes and six hours for 18 holes.

Some people say the game takes time to play because it is difficult to learn. Others argue that the better golfer is faster than the poorer golfer. Neither of these points are true. You can play the game in the correct amount of time, regardless of your golf skill. *Lack of awareness of the responsibility of each golfer is a major cause for slow play.* Furthermore, many golfers do not realize how long they are actually taking.

When playing golf, you should follow the *"Keep Pace Principle."* With this principle you should keep pace with the group in front of you, not just stay in front of the group behind you. If a group starts eight minutes before you, then you should finish just eight minutes after them. The goal is to play the game in a reasonable amount of time. You need not rush around the golf course. Each group should play in the proper amount of time, since one slow group of golfers can back-up the entire golf course. Listed on the following page are some time saving tips to help you play in the proper amount of time. *Remember, you should play 9 holes in two hours or less, and 18 holes in four hours or less.*

TIME SAVING HINTS

Appoint A Team Captain

Designate one person in your group to monitor your time on each hole.

Know The Rules Of The Game

Knowing the rules of the game will save you time on the course. You should keep a copy of the U.S.G.A. rule book in your golf bag at all times.

Minimize Practice Swings

Only one practice swing is necessary per shot.

Be Ready To Hit When It Is Your Turn

1. Plan your shot and select your club when you are approaching the ball.

2. When possible, take practice swings and get ready while others are playing their shot.

3. On the green, line up your putt before it is your turn. Also, continue putting until you have finished the hole, unless you will step on another player's line.

Don't Waste Time

1. Walk quickly to your ball.

2. Watch your shots and your playing partners shots until they stop moving, and mark the location of the ball with a landmark so that you do not lose the ball.

3. Go directly to the next tee after completing each hole.

4. If you have the honor on the next tee, make it a point to be ready first.

5. Never record your scores on, or next to, the green. You may do this at the next tee.

6. When approaching the green, leave your equipment on the side of the green closest to the next tee.

7. Give "instructions" on the practice range, not on the course.

8. Carry an extra ball, tee and ball marker in your pocket.

9. If you have to leave your power cart on the cart path, then bring extra clubs when going to hit your ball, so you don't have to go back to the cart to change clubs.

10. If you think your shot may be *lost* or *out-of-bounds*, then hit an extra ball, called a *provisional ball*, before going to look for your ball.

11. Do not spend too much time looking for lost balls. You're allowed up to five minutes to search for the ball, however, you may only want to spend one or two minutes.

5

RULES FOR AN ENJOYABLE GAME OF GOLF

When playing in a tournament or competition, there are standard rules that each player must follow. The United States Golf Association, U.S.G.A., is the governing body for golf in the United States, while the Royal & Ancient Golf Club of St. Andrews, R. & A., is the governing body in Europe. The U.S.G.A. and the R. & A. publish a book, *"The Rules of Golf,"* which is recommended if you wish to play in any golf events or if you want to expand your knowledge of the game.

There are different formats of competition for playing the game of golf. The rules of the game will vary with each competition. The two most common types of competition are *stroke-play* and *match-play*. Today, most tournaments are played with a stroke-play format, where a field of golfers play a predetermined number of holes, and the player with the lowest total score is the winner. Since this is the most common type of competition, we will explain the following rules of the game assuming a stroke-play competition. In a match-play format, one golfer plays against another. The winner of the match is the golfer that receives the lowest score on the most holes.

Many golfers play the game for years without learning the rules. You do not need to be an expert at the rules. However, you need to follow some guidelines to enjoy the game of golf. Many beginners are hesitant to play with other golfers because they do not understand the rules of the game. Furthermore, when first starting the game, the rules can be very difficult to understand or interpret. So, we will discuss some rules or guidelines to follow so that you can play an enjoyable game of golf with anybody. Again, if you intend to play competitive golf, you should purchase "The Rules of Golf".

FROM THE TEEING GROUND

1. When starting each hole, the ball may be placed on a tee and must be placed between the two tee markers. You may place the ball up to *two club-lengths* behind the tee markers, *but not in front of them.* Figure 5.1.

[Figure 5.1]
Tee Boundaries

2. You may use a tee to elevate your ball only on the teeing ground. Once you take a stroke and your ball comes off the tee, you cannot put the ball back on a tee for the rest of the hole.

3. If the ball falls off the tee before you attempt to strike it, you may re-tee the ball without *penalty*.

4. If you swing at the ball and miss, commonly referred to as a *whiff*, you must count the swing as a stroke.

5. If you swing at the ball and it just rolls off the tee, you must count the stroke and play the ball as it lies.

THROUGHOUT THE COURSE

1. *During the play of the game, you are not allowed to touch or move the ball.* You must play the ball as it lies, except for special circumstances. Under these special circumstances, when the ball may be moved or dropped, you must follow specific directions. When dropping the ball, face your target and extend your arm out at shoulders height. Then drop the ball to your side as shown in figure 5.2. Whenever the rules allow you to move or drop your ball, you cannot move the ball any closer to the hole.

[Figure 5.2]
Dropping The Ball

ON THE PUTTING GREEN

1. You should not touch the path your ball will take
   except to:
   a. Repair a ball mark.
   b. Remove debris such as leafs, branches and sand
      that may interfere with your putt.
   c. Mark your ball or tap down a ball marker.

2. You are allowed to mark, lift and clean your golf ball
   on the putting green. When replacing your ball, it
   must be put back in it's original position.

3. When making a stroke on the putting green, you incur
   a two-stroke penalty if:
   a. Your ball hits another player's ball.
   b. If the flagstick is left in the hole and your ball hits
      the flagstick.

c. If the flagstick is laying on the ground and your ball hits it.

4. If you hit a shot from off the green and it comes to rest against the flagstick, but not below the level lip of the hole, your shot cannot be counted as being in the hole. If you take the flag out and the ball falls in the hole, then you have *holed out*. If the ball falls away from the hole, then you must replace the ball on the lip of the hole. There is no penalty.

YOU MAY MOVE THE BALL FOR THE FOLLOWING SITUATIONS WITHOUT A PENALTY

1. If your ball lands in standing water that is not marked as a hazard, you may drop the ball at the closest dry location but not closer to the hole. For instance, if it has been raining, or a sprinkler is on in the fairway, and your ball is in a puddle of water in the center of the fairway, then you do not have to hit your ball from within the puddle. If the ball is in the bunker, you can move it, but you must still keep it within the bunker.

2. If there are areas of the golf course under repair, such as an irrigation line, dead tree, etc., and your ball comes to rest within this area, then you may drop the ball outside of this area, but no closer to the hole.

3. Sometimes man-made objects of different sizes and shapes interfere with your *ball, stance* or *swing*. If the object is moveable, like a rope, hose, paper cup, or yardage stake, then move the object to take your shot and replace it after your shot. If you cannot move the object and it interferes with your ball, stance or swing, then find the nearest point of relief and drop

the ball within one club-length, but still no closer to the hole. For instance, if your ball lands on or next to a cart path, bench, tee sign, ball washer, etc., then you may move your ball according to the rule. Some man-made objects are considered a normal part of the golf course, such as a bridge or stone wall. In this case you would not get relief. When playing in a competition, the committee will determine which objects you can and cannot get relief from.

4. If a hole made by an animal interferes with your ball, stance or swing, then you may move your ball one club-length, but no nearer the hole.

5. While playing, if you hit your ball from off the green and it hits another player's ball while at rest, play your next shot from where your ball lands, and replace the other player's ball to its original position. There is no penalty. Figure 5.3.

PENALTIES

Improving Position Of Your Ball, Stance Or Swing
You may not improve the position of your ball, stance or swing by moving, bending or breaking anything growing. This includes objects such as grass, branches, leaves, and roots that may be in your way. If you do, this is a two-stroke penalty, which means that you must add two strokes to your score. If an object is not growing and interferes with your ball, stance or swing, such as grass clippings, dead branches or leaves, you can move the object so that it does not interfere. However, if you are in a water hazard or bunker, you may not touch or move any objects.

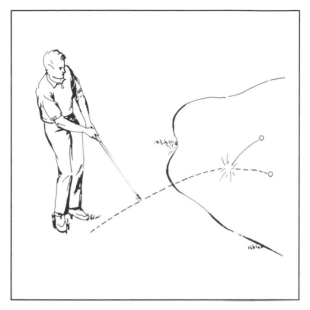

[Figure 5.3]
Hitting Another Player's Ball

Playing The Wrong Ball

If you play the wrong ball, you must inform your fellow golfers and go back to your original ball, and finish the hole with your original ball. This is a two-stroke penalty, but you do not have to count the strokes you played with the other ball.

Ball Lost Or Out-Of-Bounds

If your ball is lost or out-of-bounds, you must go back to where you played your last shot from, and continue to play from that location. You must count the shot you hit out-of-bounds or lost, and add a one-stroke penalty before you hit your next shot.

Ball In Water Hazard

If your ball goes into a *water hazard,* first determine what type of hazard you hit your ball into. There are two types of hazards, *regular water hazards* and *lateral water hazards.* Regular water hazards are defined with yellow stakes, and lateral water hazards are defined with red stakes. The difference between the two is how you would get *relief* from the hazards if your ball goes into them.

REGULAR WATER HAZARD

As shown in figure 5.4, if your ball lands in a regular water hazard you have three options.

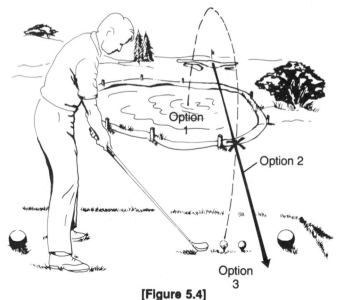

Option 1

Option 2

Option 3

[Figure 5.4]
Relief From A Regular Water Hazard

1. If you think you can play the ball as it lies, then you may do so without a penalty stroke.

2. If the ball is not playable, mark the point at which the ball entered the hazard, and keep this point between you and the flag when you play your next

stroke. You may go as far away from the flag as you want. You must count the shot that you hit into the hazard, and add a one-stroke penalty to your score.

3. You may play another shot from where you hit your last shot. You must count the shot that you hit into the hazard and add a one-stroke penalty to your score.

LATERAL WATER HAZARD

Sometimes it is not practical to keep the point where the ball entered the hazard between you and the target. Therefore, in addition to the three options you have when playing from a regular water hazard, there are two additional options to get relief from a lateral water hazard. As shown in figure 5.5, your additional options include:

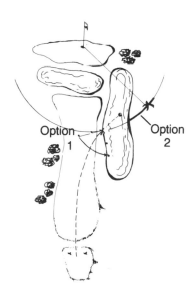

[Figure 5.5]
Relief From A Lateral Water Hazard

1. You may play the ball from within two club-lengths of where the ball entered the hazard, but no closer to the hole. You must count the shot that you hit into the hazard, and add a one-stroke penalty to your score.

2. You may play the ball on the opposite side of the hazard, an equal distance from the target. You must count the shot that you hit into the hazard, and add a one-stroke penalty to your score.

Ball Unplayable

If your ball comes to rest where it may be difficult or impossible to hit, for example, against a tree or in a bush, then you may take a one-stroke penalty with three options as shown in figure 5.6. Regardless of which option you choose, you must count the original shot, and add a penalty stroke before your next shot.

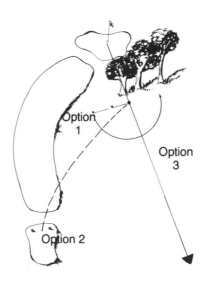

[Figure 5.6]
Relief From An Unplayable Lie

1. Drop the ball within two club-lengths of its original position, but not closer to the hole.

2. Play from where you hit your last shot.

3. Keep the point of the ball between you and the target going back as far as you would like.

6

WHAT DETERMINES BALL FLIGHT

Before we address the fundamentals of the golf swing, let's first take a look at what makes the ball fly as it does. How do we get the proper ball flight? Many golfers get so involved in the technical aspects of the golf swing that they never ask themselves what determines the flight of the golf ball.

At impact, which is the point when the club meets the ball, if the club hits the lower half of the golf ball, the ball will go in the air. If the club hits the top half of the ball, the ball will go along the ground. Figure 6.1.

A. Hitting the top half of the ball.

Club Path

Ball Flight

[Figure 6.1]
Ball Flight

B. Hitting the ball and turf at the same time.

Ball Flight

Club Path

C. Hitting the turf before the ball.

Club Path

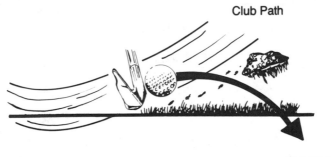

Ball Flight

[Figure 6.1]
Ball Flight

You do not need to help the ball up when hitting it. A golf club is designed so the angle (loft) of the clubface will automatically lift the ball in the air. Many beginners believe that you should not hit the grass when playing golf. This is false. In order to get the ball airborne, you must swing the club down to or below the ball. Therefore, when using your irons, you may hit the ball, then continue your swing down through the grass. With your woods, you should not continue down through the grass.

There are two variables that affect the direction of your golf shot, *the position of your clubface at impact* and *the path or direction of your swing*. The position of the clubface can either be *square, open* or *closed* as illustrated in figure 6.2. There are also three different swing paths as shown in figure 6.3. By combining these two variables there are nine different directions your ball can travel. Figure 6.3.

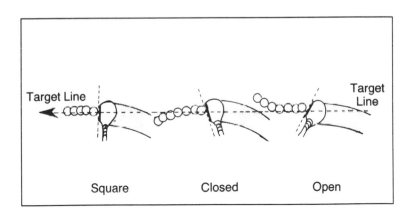

[Figure 6.2]
Angle of Clubface at Impact

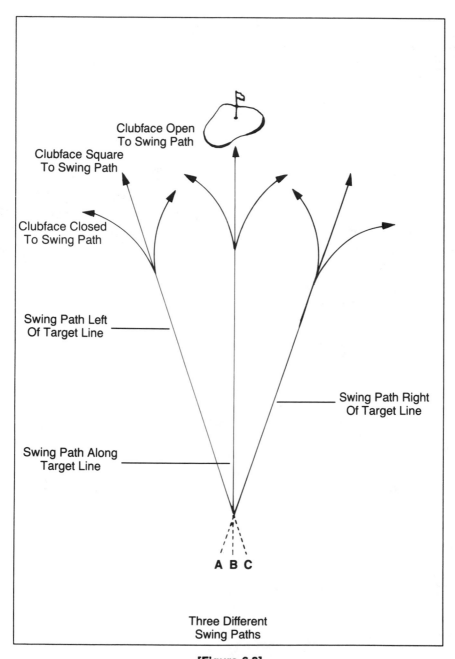

[Figure 6.3]
The Nine Possible Ball Flights

As shown in figure 6.4, for a right handed golfer, a shot that goes straight left is called a *pull shot,* a shot that curves slightly to the left is called a *draw,* and a severe curve to the left is called a *hook.* A shot that goes straight right is called a *push shot,* a shot that curves slightly to the right is called a *fade,* and a severe curve to the right is called a *slice.* Frequently, golfers' shots tend to curve to the right. If you are getting started and experience this problem, remember you are not alone.

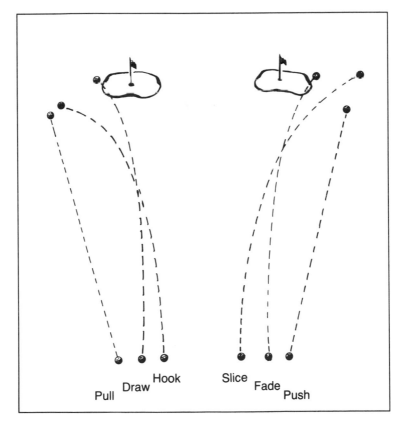

[Figure 6.4]
Different Types of Shots

7

THE PRE-SWING - THE GRIP

The first six chapters were designed to introduce you to the game of golf and get you prepared to play the game. Now it is time to learn how to swing the club, along with how to play the different shots used in the game. When learning each shot, it is important that you do not try to learn everything at once. Learn one or two fundamentals at a time. Focus on additional fundamentals only after you become comfortable with the previous ones. Active participation is also recommended. Over the next few chapters, you will find it helpful to put yourself into the same body positions as shown in the illustrations. To see what position you are in, it is helpful to practice in front of a mirror.

To understand the golf swing, you must start with the basics involved in preparing for the swing. Throughout this book these fundamentals will be referred to as the *pre-swing fundamentals*. This means before the swing, and includes the *grip, posture, ball position,* and *alignment.* Your pre-swing fundamentals directly affect the success of your swing. They are the building blocks to a good golf swing. Only with proper pre-swing fundamentals can you develop a consistent golf swing.

How you hold the club, also referred to as the *grip,* is very important. Yet it is often overlooked. Therefore, we will use this entire chapter to discuss how to grip the club.

In Chapter 6, we mentioned that the angle of the clubface at impact affects the flight of the golf ball. It is important to know that the angle of the clubface is directly affected by your grip. The grip is the only link, or connection, between your body and the golf club. So, as you change your grip, you change the angle of your clubface.

HOW FIRMLY TO GRIP THE CLUB

You should grip the club just firmly enough to control it. Many golfers are not consistent because they grip the club too tightly. While gripping the club, imagine the grip as a small bird. When holding this bird you would want to hold it tight enough to control it's movement, but you would not want to choke it.

The faster you can swing the golf club, the farther the golf ball will travel. The energy your body generates to swing the golf club is transferred to the club through your hands. If there is too much tension in your hands, you will reduce the speed the club can travel. *Too much tension reduces clubhead speed, limiting tension increases clubhead speed.* Imagine how difficult it would be to steer a bike or automobile if you gripped the handle bars or steering wheel too tightly.

There are two major reasons people often grip the golf club too tightly. First, they associate power and distance with a firm grip. Second, people are often nervous when playing, which adds tension to their hands. Relax your hands to reduce grip pressure. This will help you develop a better swing.

TYPES OF GRIPS

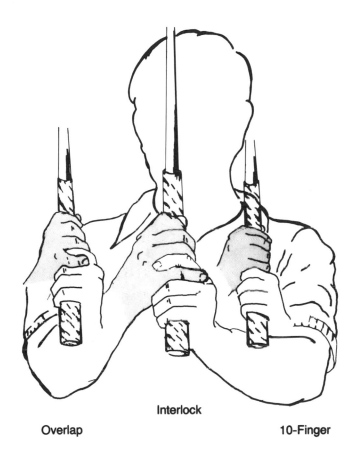

Interlock

Overlap   10-Finger

[Figure 7.1]
Types of Grips

When playing golf, you may use one of three grips to hold the golf club: the *overlap,* the *interlock,* or the *10-finger* grip as shown in figure 7.1. Each of the three grips discussed are similar except for the placement of the index finger of the left hand and the little finger of the right hand. Each of the three grips have proven successful at the professional level.

The overlap grip is the most common grip, with approximately 60 percent of all golfers using this type. With this grip, the little finger of the right hand rests on or overlaps the index finger of the left hand. If you elect to use the overlap grip, make sure that the little finger on your right hand is hooked in the groove between the index finger and middle finger of your left hand. This will help keep the hands from slipping apart, and make the hands feel like one unit.

The second most common grip is the interlock grip, with approximately 30 percent of all golfers using this type of grip. Both the overlap and the interlock grips promote a feeling of unity by having the fingers overlapping or interlocking. These grips are best for people with average or large hand size and strength.

The third grip is the 10-finger grip, with approximately 10 percent of all golfers using this grip. The 10-finger grip is recommended for men and women with small hands or fingers. Figure 7.2 will help determine which grip is best for you, based on your glove size. Your strength and individual preference will also affect the grip you choose.

GLOVE SIZE	MEN	WOMEN
Cadet Small	10-finger	N/A
Small	any	10-finger
Cadet Medium	any	N/A
Medium	overlap or interlock	any
Cadet Large	overlap or interlock	N/A
Large	overlap or interlock	overlap or interlock
X-Large	overlap	overlap or interlock

[Figure 7.2]
Guide To Selecting A Grip
(Cadet Gloves Are Not Available In Women's Sizes.
Check With A Local Golf Professional To Assure A Proper Fit.)

Next, we will review a simple routine to help you develop a proper grip. Carefully follow each step.

THE LEFT HAND

Step 1

While bending at the waist, hold the grip end of the club with your right hand. Let your left arm hang down and out in front of you. Your left hand should be about 4 to 6 inches from your body, with your fingers pointing directly to the ground. Figure 7.3.

[Figure 7.3]

Step 2

Place the club on an angle across your left hand so the shaft is pressed against the muscular pad of your palm and lies across the first or second joint of the forefinger. Figure 7.4.

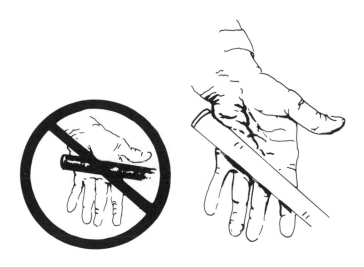

[Figure 7.4]

Step 3

Now lightly close your fingers around the club. The last three fingers of your left hand should control the club. Figure 7.5.

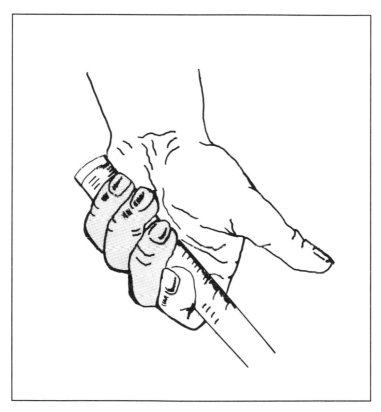

[Figure 7.5]

Step 4

As shown in figure 7.6, put your thumb on the right side of the center of the grip. You should now see two or three knuckles in your left hand. If you do not, then you must check that the club is not into your palm too much rather than your fingers, and that your thumb is on the right side of the center of the grip.

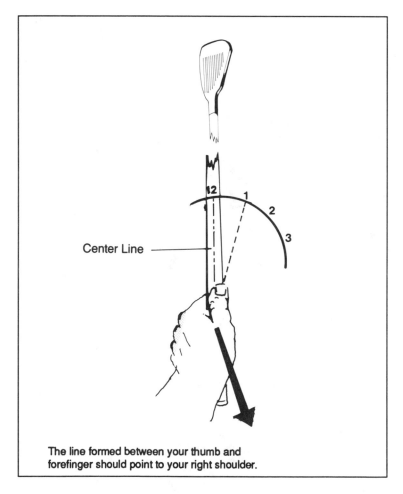

Center Line

The line formed between your thumb and forefinger should point to your right shoulder.

[Figure 7.6]

The correct position of your thumb is important because your *left thumb supports the club at the top of your backswing.* Do not let your thumb go too far to the right side of center so that it is no longer on the golf club.

To illustrate the importance of the left thumb on the shaft, properly grip a club with just your left hand. Next, place your hand and the club over your right shoulder as illustrated in figure 7.7. Now, do the same thing, but without your thumb on the shaft. You should feel a difference in the control of the golf club when it is above your shoulder.

The left thumb supports the club
at the top of the backswing

[Figure 7.7]
Correct Thumb Position

RIGHT HAND

Step 1

When placing the club in your right hand, the shaft should be placed along the fingers, not the palm of the right hand, as illustrated in figure 7.8. This is also the point where you will alter the position of the index finger of your left hand, and the little finger of your right hand, depending on which grip you use as illustrated in figure 7.1.

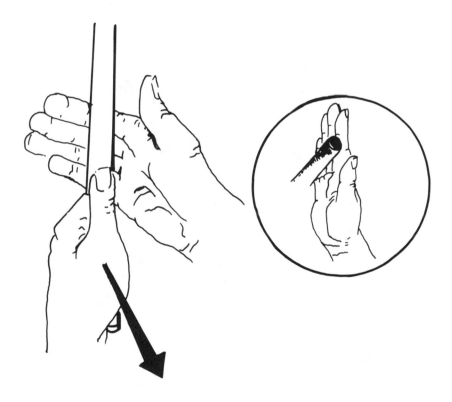

[Figure 7.8]

Step 2

Next, lightly close your fingers around the club. The club should be controlled primarily by the two middle fingers. Figure 7.9.

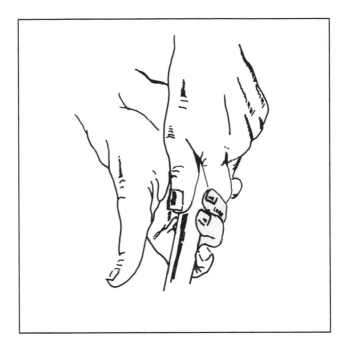

[Figure 7.9]

Step 3

Now, your right thumb should be placed just to the left side of the center of the shaft as illustrated in figure 7.10. As a result, the palm of your right hand will cover your left thumb. Remember, it is important that both thumbs should be on the shaft of the golf club. The left thumb should be just to the right side of center and the right thumb just to the left side of center.

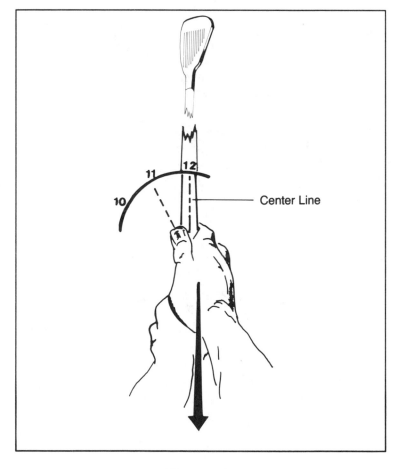

[Figure 7.10]

Going through just a few simple steps, you have now developed a good fundamental grip as shown in figure 7.11. To help make this grip a regular part of your pre-swing fundamentals, practice this routine for the grip 10 to 15 minutes per day for one to two weeks.

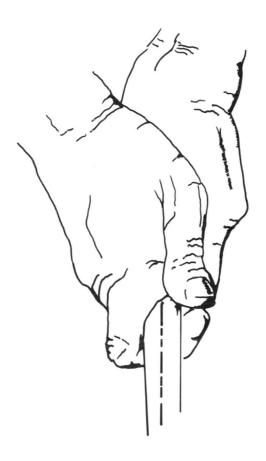

[Figure 7.11]

8

THE PRE-SWING - POSTURE, BALL POSITION & ALIGNMENT

To develop a consistent golf swing, you must also learn the remaining pre-swing fundamentals; *posture, ball position*, and *alignment*. These fundamentals are very important when setting up to take your shot. The fundamentals discussed in this chapter will apply to normal full-swing shots with either your woods or irons. The pre-swing fundamentals change for the various shots around the green and will be discussed with each shot in Chapters 10 and 11.

POSTURE

[Figure 8.1]
Posture

Posture, also referred to as *stance*, is the position you put your body into when setting up to hit the ball. Figure 8.1. Setting up to the ball is also referred to as *addressing* the ball. Your posture is the foundation or base of the golf swing. Good posture is important in order to develop maximum power during the swing.

When setting up to hit the ball, the inside of your feet should be approximately shoulder-width apart. Figure 8.2. When using your shorter irons (7,8,9 and wedges), you may narrow your stance slightly. Your weight should be evenly distributed on the balls of your feet. Figure 8.3 shows your right foot should be perpendicular to your target line, while your left foot should be turned a quarter turn to the left.

[Figure 8.2]
The inside of your feet should be shoulder width, except when using your short irons (7,8,9 and wedges), then you may narrow your stance the width of one foot.

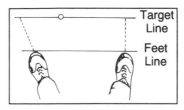

[Figure 8.3]
Position of Feet at Address

Some golfers experience difficulty developing good posture when beginning the game. Therefore, a number of illustrations are included to help you visualize and feel the correct posture or stance. To help visualize your posture, practice in front of a mirror or with a video camera.

Posture Check Points

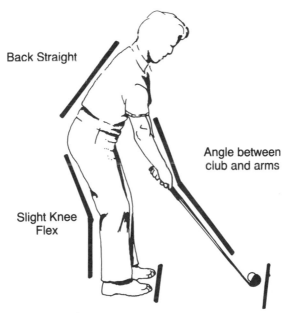

Back Straight

Angle between club and arms

Slight Knee Flex

Weight evenly distributed on the balls of both feet

Hands 4 to 6 inches from body

[Figure 8.4]
Posture Check Points

Three Steps To Good Posture

The following illustrations provide a simple three-step approach to developing good posture.

STEP 1

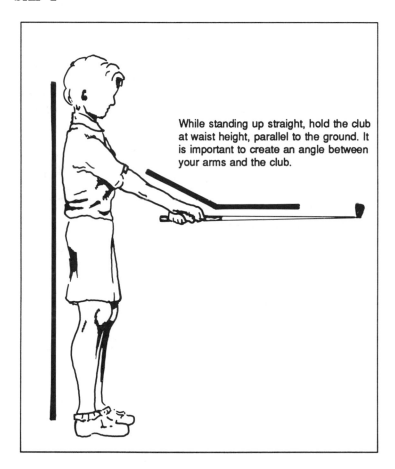

While standing up straight, hold the club at waist height, parallel to the ground. It is important to create an angle between your arms and the club.

[Figure 8.5]

STEP **2**

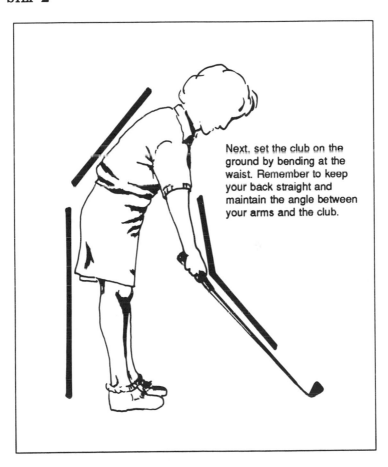

Next, set the club on the ground by bending at the waist. Remember to keep your back straight and maintain the angle between your arms and the club.

[Figure 8.6]

STEP 3

Last, flex your knees slightly.

[Figure 8.7]

Common Posture Faults

Incorrect posture reduces your chance of executing a good golf shot. The following illustrations show some common posture faults which lead to the following:

1. Too much tension in your hands and arms.
2. Overuse of your hands during the swing.
3. Poor balance.
4. Incorrect use of your legs during the swing.

[Figure 8.8]
Fault - The arms and club form a straight line.

[Figure 8.9]
Fault - The back is hunched

[Figure 8.10]
Fault - The knees are not flexed

[Figure 8.11]

Fault - The knees are flexed too much

[Figure 8.12]

Fault - Reaching too far at set-up

Proper Hand Position

As shown if figure 8.13, when addressing the golf ball, your hands should be in a relaxed position just left of the center of your body. You will feel like your hands are extending out from the inside of your left leg. Figure 8.14 shows the hands too far left of center, and too far right of center.

[Figure 8.13]
Correct Arm & Hand Position at Address

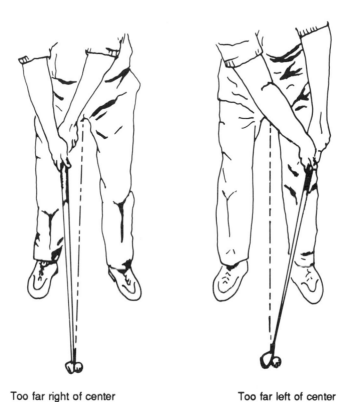

Too far right of center   Too far left of center

[Figure 8.14]
Incorrect Arm & Hand Position at Address

Proper Arm and Elbow Position

Do not put your elbows too close together when addressing the ball. This will add unwanted tension to your upper arms and restrict your arm swing. Simply let your arms hang down in a relaxed manner. Figure 8.15.

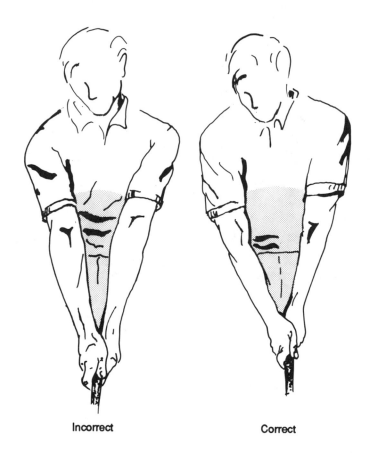

Incorrect   Correct

[Figure 8.15]
Your arms and elbows should not be too close together at address.

BALL POSITION

Ball position is the relationship between the golf ball and your feet when addressing the ball. Figure 8.16. There are different theories concerning where the ball should be placed in relation to your feet. We will follow a simple guide for proper ball position. Starting with the driver, the ball should be on a line directly off the heel of your left foot. For fairway wood shots, the ball is moved 2 inches toward the center of your body. For all iron shots the ball should be an additional 1 or 2 inches toward the center of your body. Make sure that for a normal shot, you never play the ball to the right side of the center of your body.

The distance you stand from the ball is automatically determined by your posture and the length of the club. The longer the club, the farther you will stand from the ball. When bending over to the ball, your arms should be comfortably extended. The grip end of the golf club should be approximately 4 to 6 inches away from your legs.

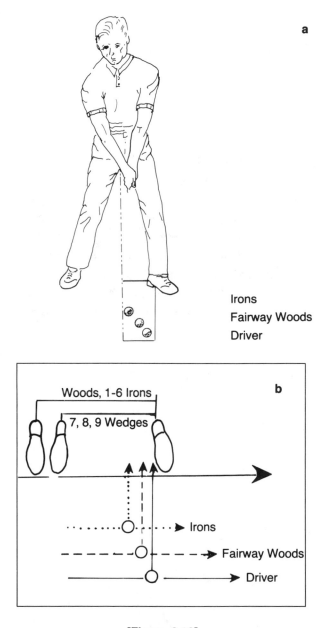

a

Irons
Fairway Woods
Driver

Woods, 1-6 Irons

7, 8, 9 Wedges

b

Irons

Fairway Woods

Driver

[Figure 8.16]
Ball Position

ALIGNMENT

Unfortunately, most golfers align their club and body incorrectly to the target when setting up to strike the ball. This leads to inconsistent golf shots. There are, however, a few simple principles to follow for proper alignment. First, as shown in figure 8.17, the clubhead should be placed along the *target line,* with the leading edge of the clubface perpendicular to, or at a 90 degree angle to the target line.

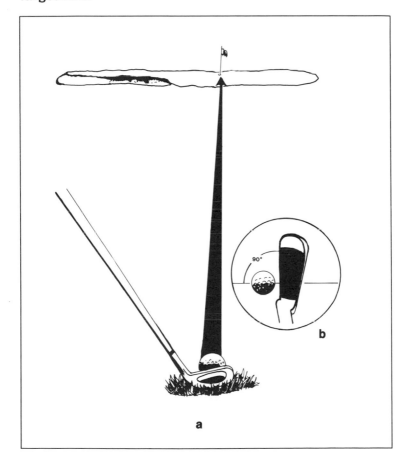

[Figure 8.17]
Proper Alignment of the Clubhead to the Target Line

Second, as shown in figure 8.18, you should line up your body left of the target line. *Do not aim your body directly at your target.* The only line that should be aligned to your target is the target line. As you increase the distance between you and the target, aim your body further to the left of the target.

Shoulder Line

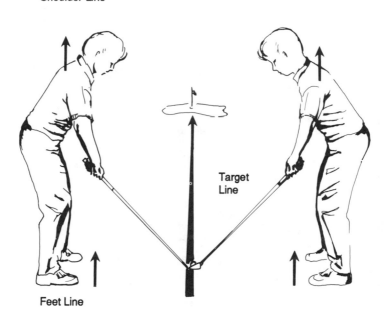

Target Line

Feet Line

Right-handed golfer   Left-handed golfer

Align your body parallel to the target, not directly to your target.

[Figure 8.18]
Alignment

Last, when setting up to play different shots, it is necessary to adjust your stance. For a normal full-swing shot you should use a *square* stance, so your feet will line up parallel to your target line. Figure 8.19b. When playing most shots near the green, you should use an *open* stance. Figure 8.19c. These shots will be discussed in further detail in Chapter 11.

As you play the game more, you will find it helpful to learn how to curve the ball for selected shots. To make a shot draw or hook, you should *close* your stance. Figure 8.19a. To fade or slice a shot, you should open your stance. Figure 8.19c.

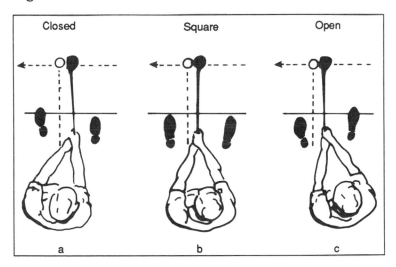

[Figure 8.19]
Different Stances

9

THE FULL SWING - WOODS AND IRONS

What makes the game of golf so exciting? Well, one of the most enjoyable parts of playing the game is the self-satisfaction that accompanies a well-played golf shot. We have covered all of the pre-swing fundamentals - the grip, posture, ball position, and alignment. Now it is time to discuss the golf swing.

Many golfers view the golf swing as a complex sequence of movements in an attempt to hit a golf ball. In this chapter we will address the various fundamentals of the golf swing. This should answer many of your questions about the swing, and help you to develop a simple approach. Do not try to learn all of the information discussed in this section at once. Practice only one or two fundamentals at a time. When making a golf swing, many golfers try to focus on too many things, thus making the swing too technical. It only takes between two to three seconds to make a golf swing, *so keep the swing as simple as possible.*

For instructional purposes, we will discuss the swing in two separate parts, starting with the *backswing* and then discussing the *forward swing.* When actually making your swing these two movements become one continuous motion.

THE BACKSWING

The *backswing* includes all movements from the point you start the golf swing, until the club starts going back down toward the golf ball. Figure 9.1a through 9.1e.

a

The hands, arms, and shoulders
should start the swing as a unit.

[Figure 9.1]
The Backswing

The Take Away

The *takeaway* is the start of the golf swing. When starting the swing you should feel the hands, arms and shoulders starting the swing at the same time, as a unit. This is referred to as a *one-piece takeaway*. Figure 9.1. In reality, the hands start just a split-second before the arms, the arms start a split-second before the shoulders, and the shoulders a split-second before the hips.

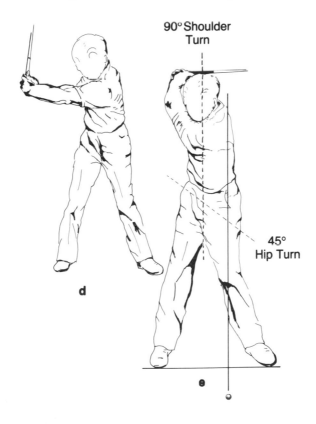

At the top of the backswing, most of your body should be right of the ball.

During the first 12 to 18 inches of the backswing, it is important to feel as though the club is dragging along the ground. Figure 9.2. A common fault for many beginners is that they pick the club up from the ground with their hands too quickly, rather than letting the club come off the ground naturally. If you start the swing with your hands, arms and shoulders as a unit, the club will drag back along the ground, then automatically come off the ground.

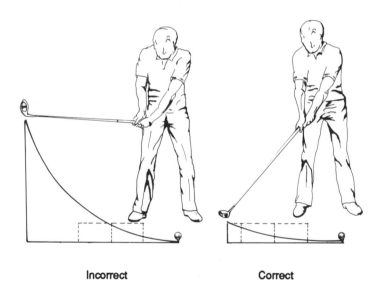

Incorrect   Correct

[Figure 9.2]
The Takeaway

Weight Transfer & Footwork

When addressing the golf ball, your weight should be equally distributed on each foot. Figure 9.1a. During the backswing the distribution of the weight on your right foot increases. At the top of the backswing, you should have 80 to 90 percent of the weight on your right foot and 10 to

20 percent of the weight on your opposite foot. Figure 9.1e. Your power in the golf swing is generated by properly transferring your weight back away from the target on the backswing, then transferring your weight toward the target on the forward swing.

At the top of the backswing, if you were to draw a line from the golf ball and extend it upwards, most of your body would be behind the golf ball. Figure 9.1e. This illustrates that you must have your weight behind the golf ball before you can drive forward toward the target.

DURING THE BACKSWING

As you turn your shoulders in the backswing, your left foot, knee, and hip move toward your right leg. The outside of your left foot may come off the ground a few inches, while the front inside edge of your left foot should stay on the ground. Figure 9.3.

[Figure 9.3]
During the backswing the left hip, knee
and foot move toward the right foot.

Like other sports, it is important to develop good balance and footwork. Your right leg plays a vital role in developing this balance and footwork. During the entire backswing, your right leg must maintain the same angle it had at the address position. Figure 9.4. You must keep the weight on the inside of your right leg and foot. This means that your right knee cannot bow out, allowing the weight to be on the outside of your right foot. To maintain proper balance in any sport, you must always keep the weight on the inside edge of your feet.

Incorrect   Correct

[Figure 9.4]
The right leg should maintain the
same angle throughout the backswing.

The Top Of The Backswing

To assure a consistent forward swing, it only makes sense to first be in the proper position at the top of the backswing. At the top of the backswing, the club should never go past parallel to the ground. Figure 9.5a. Any movement past parallel can lead to difficulty in maintaining balance, and timing the return of the golf club to the ball.

The shoulders should turn 90 degrees, while the hips turn approximately 45 degrees. You should feel your left shoulder just under your chin. Figure 9.5a. A common problem during the golf swing is an incorrect shoulder turn. Figure 9.5b shows how a poor shoulder turn leads to a poor weight transfer, because the weight stays on the left leg during the backswing.

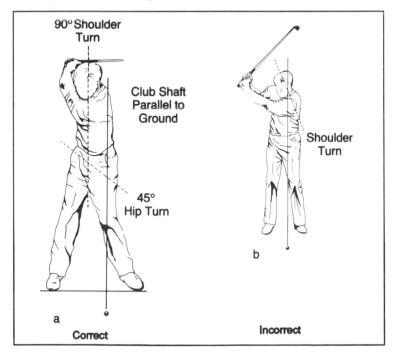

[Figure 9.5]
Your shoulders should turn 90 degrees during the backswing.

At the top of the backswing, it is also important to have your hands and wrist in the proper position. First, your wrist should be cocked, or *hinged,* to generate maximum clubhead speed in the golf swing. Figure 9.6. To demonstrate the importance of properly hinging your wrist, try hitting some balls while keeping your wrist perfectly still throughout the swing. Then try hitting some balls while allowing your wrist to hinge. You will notice increased distance from your shots if you allow your wrist to hinge.

[Figure 9.6]
Proper Wrist Position at the Top of the Backswing

The angle of your wrist and hands at the top of your backswing are also important to properly control the club during the swing. Figure 9.7 illustrates the correct position for your wrist to be in at the top of the backswing.

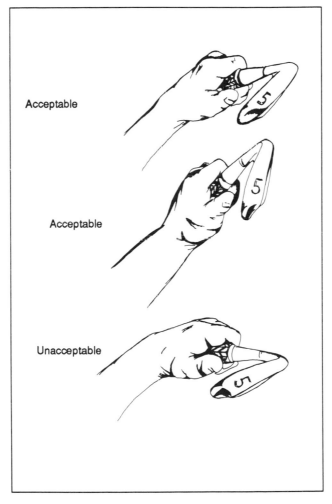

[Figure 9.7]
Proper Angle of Your Hands and Wrist at the Top of Your Backswing

Many golfers never get the club into the proper position at the top of the backswing. This is normally a result of starting the swing incorrectly. Therefore, two drills will be discussed later in this chapter, the *thumbs-up drill* and the *half-swing drill,* to make sure that you start the first half of the backswing correctly. This will also help you get the club into the proper position throughout the swing.

THE FORWARD SWING

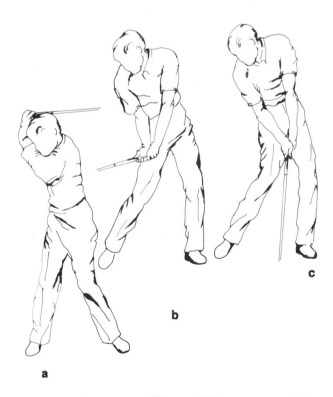

[Figure 9.8]
The Forward Swing

The *forward swing* is the movement toward the target, starting from the top of the backswing and going to the finish position of the golf swing. Figure 9.8. A good forward swing is the result of good pre-swing fundamentals and having a proper backswing. Do not stop your swing between your backswing and forward swing. *The golf swing is one continuous motion.*

d   e

Arm Swing

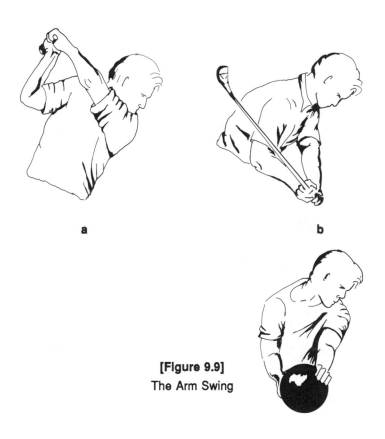

a   b

[Figure 9.9]
The Arm Swing

During the forward swing, the arms and hands swing from over your right shoulder, down to the ball, then over your left shoulder. The arm swing is very important, because the faster you can swing your arms, *the faster the club will travel,* therefore making your shots go farther. The

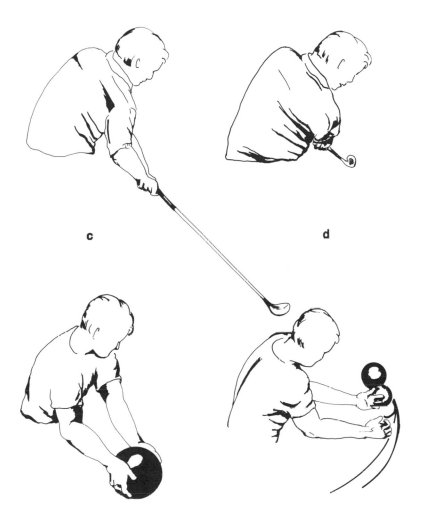

arm swing should resemble throwing a ball with two hands, or a two-handed backhand in tennis. Do not try to just hit the ball. Develop an arm swing that will continue past the point of impact with the ball and finish over your left shoulder. Figure 9.9.

Weight Transfer And Footwork

Some golfers often wonder how a shorter person can hit the ball great distances. The answer is, with good timing and a proper weight transfer, your arms will swing faster. A good weight transfer increases the momentum of your body toward your target. The same is true for all other sports where you must propel an object from one point to another. Imagine trying to throw or hit a baseball while keeping your legs perfectly still. You would not be able to throw or hit the ball very far without feeling awkward. This is because you need to transfer your weight toward your target when throwing or batting in baseball. During the golf swing, as your arms swing forward, the weight distribution between your feet will also change. When starting the forward swing, 80 to 90 percent of the weight

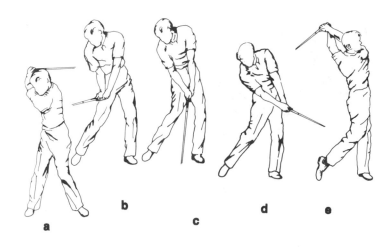

[Figure 9.10]
The Weight Transfer in the Forward Swing

should be on your right foot. At impact, your weight should be evenly distributed between your feet. When you get to the finish position in the golf swing, you should have at least 90 percent of your weight on your left foot. To help initiate the weight transfer for the forward swing, you should push off with your right foot. Figures 9.10a through 9.10e illustrate the weight transfer and footwork during the forward swing.

The Finish Position

[Figure 9.11]
The Proper Finish Position

The position your body should be in after swinging the club is referred to as the *finish position.* Figure 9.11. In the finish position you should:

a. Have your hands and arms over your left shoulder.
b. Have your chest and stomach facing the target, as your body rotates during the forward swing.
c. Have just the toe of your right foot on the ground, as your right knee and foot move toward the target.

The majority of your weight should now be on your left foot. A common problem for many beginning and inter-mediate golfers is that they do not transfer their weight properly. As a result, they do not get into a correct finish position.   After hitting a shot, you should be able to stay in the finish position for three seconds, or until the ball has landed. Try this when you are practicing by counting to yourself. You should be able to stay in the finish position without losing your balance.

THE THUMBS-UP DRILL

Many golfers do not start the golf swing, or take-away, correctly. The *thumbs-up drill* is designed to assure a correct take-away, therefore, making the full-swing easier.

At waist height in the backswing and forward swing, the thumbs should be pointing directly to the sky in a vertical position.

a   b

[Figure 9.12]
Thumbs-up Drill

You will not use a club in this drill. As shown in figure 9.12, take your hands and arms to waist height, or slightly above, in the backswing. At waist height both thumbs should point up toward the sky. For the forward swing, bring your hands forward, making sure that your thumbs are pointing towards the sky at waist height, also. Practice these movements, making sure your thumbs are in the proper position, so when you are making your swing with a club, you are familiar with where your hands and thumbs should be.

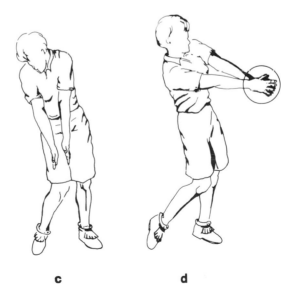

c   d

THE HALF-SWING DRILL

The *half-swing drill* is also designed to do the same thing as the thumbs-up drill. As shown in figure 9.13, at waist height in the backswing and forward swing, the toe of the golf club should be pointing toward the sky. A common error for beginning golfers is that they take the club

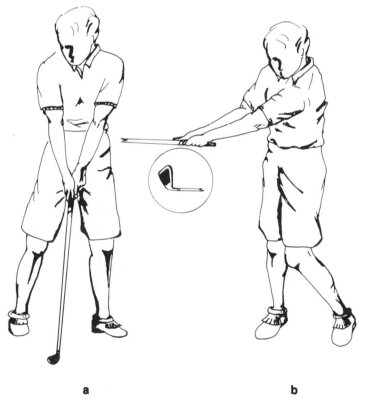

a   b

At waist height in the backswing and forward swing, the toe of the club should be pointing directly to the sky.

[Figure 9.13]
Half Swing Drill

back in a *closed* position during the backswing. Figure 9.14. This makes it very difficult to take a full-swing and control the club at the top of the backswing. Do this drill slowly so that you can check the toe position and get the feel of how the club will feel during the swing.

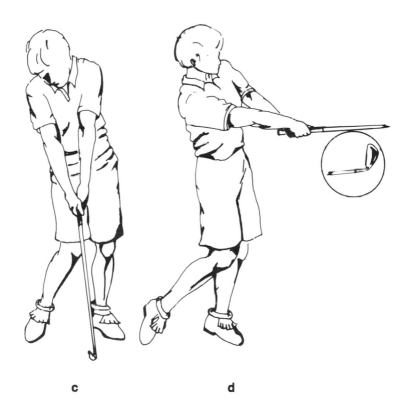

c   d

a   Correct

b   Closed/Incorrect

c   Open/Incorrect

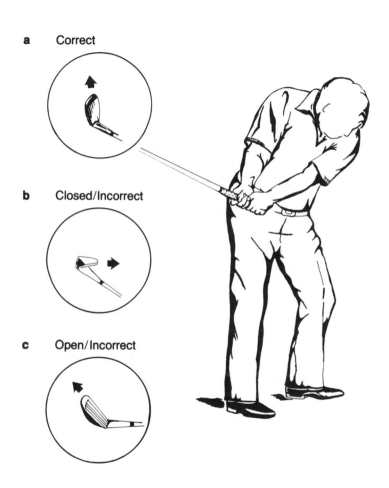

It is very important to have the club in the
correct position at waist height in the backswing.

[Figure 9.14]
Club Position During Backswing

GENERAL SWING TIPS

There are a few general points that also need to be discussed concerning the golf swing including: *swing balance, swing center, swing plane* and *common swing myths.*

Swing Balance

A key element in the golf swing is *balance.* Without balance, it is difficult to develop a consistent swing with maximum power. Professional golfers look like they are swinging so easily and gracefully because they are in balance. To maintain good balance in the golf swing you need a good stance, a proper weight transfer and you need to maintain your swing center.

Swing Center

To help develop consistent shot-making, you should maintain a *swing center.* Your swing center is an imaginary pole, or center, that you want to rotate your body around while swinging. To help visualize the swing center, imagine your spine and head as the swing center. Ideally, your spine and head stay stationary from the time you start the backswing until impact as shown in the illustration in figure 9.15. After impact, your head and spine should move forward from the momentum of your swing. Your body should turn or rotate around your head and spine. Most golfers do not stay perfectly centered until impact. The less movement, the better your chance for consistent golf shots.

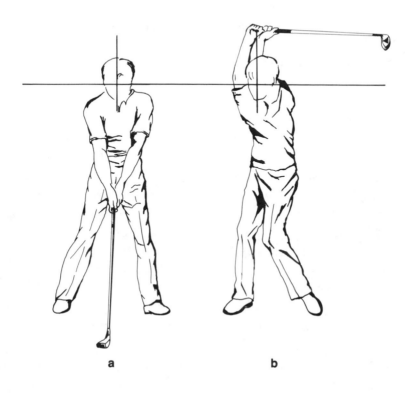

a   b

[Figure 9.15]
Swing Center

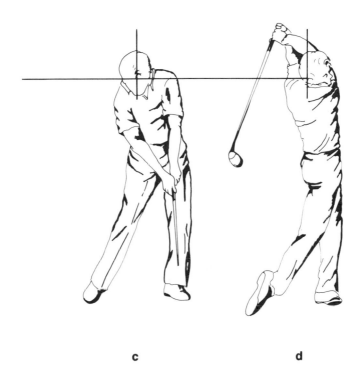

c   d

Swing Plane

The *swing plane* is an imaginary circle that you swing the club along. Swinging on the correct swing plane will also help develop consistent shot-making. The plane can be seen best by standing to the right of the golfer, as shown in figure 9.16.

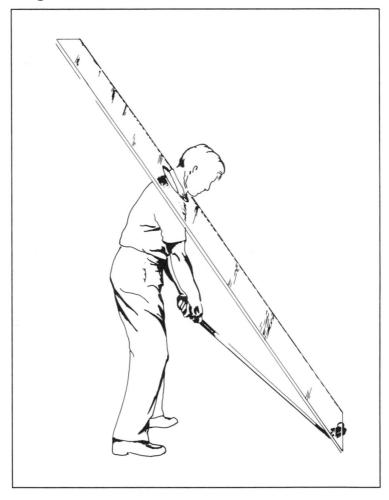

[Figure 9.16]
The Swing Plane

The swing plane will change based on the amount you have to bend your waist, or tilt your spine, to reach the ball. When using a longer club, you are standing more upright at address, therefore your swing plane will be flatter. With a short iron you will bend more at the waist, so your swing plane will be more upright. Do not try to alter your swing plane for each different club. It will change automatically as you change the tilt of your spine at address. Figure 9.17 illustrates how your swing plane automatically changes with different clubs.

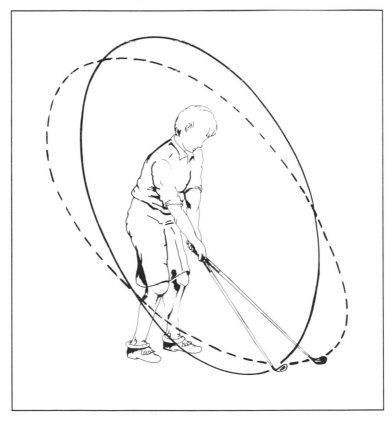

[Figure 9.17]
Different Swing Planes

Golf Swing Myths

MYTH #1 - SWING EASY

Many golfers believe you should swing easy when trying to hit the golf ball. Generally, this is false. The distance a golf ball travels is directly affected by the speed the club is traveling at impact. As a beginner, it is important to develop clubhead speed by making an aggressive swing. Now, this does not mean swing so hard that you swing out of your shoes. It means, put some effort or zip, into your golf swing. For example, when swinging a baseball bat, you do not think of swinging too hard, you think of making an aggressive swing at the baseball. Most professionals learn to hit the ball a great distance, then they learn to control the flight of the ball. When watching children learn to swing, they normally take an aggressive swing at the ball. They do not get caught up in the technical aspects of the swing. As a result, children often surprise others at how well they can hit the ball. One of the worst things you can say to anyone learning to swing the club is *"Swing easy."*

MYTH #2 - KEEP YOUR HEAD DOWN

Many beginners believe you should keep your head down throughout the swing. This is false. During the backswing and until the point of impact, you should look at the golf ball. However, after you hit the ball, the momentum of your right shoulder should force your head to turn toward your target, as illustrated back in figure 9.15. If you keep your head down after impact, you will restrict your follow through, as shown in figure 9.18.

Correct Finish

Incorrect Finish

[Figure 9.18]
Correct vs. Incorrect Finish

MYTH #3 - YOU PICKED YOUR HEAD UP

A frequently misused phrase is *"You picked your head up."* It seems whenever somebody hits a bad golf shot, somebody says, "You picked your head up." Occasionally this may be true. However, most of the time there are other reasons why the shot was not hit well. Golfers often feel they need to help get the ball into the air with an upward swing path. As a result, their club hits the top of the ball and the ball travels along the ground. The club is designed to get the ball airborne. All you need to do is swing the club below the ball and the ball will automatically go upward.

As a beginner, practice hitting shots with the ball on a tee with your irons. When swinging, aim at the tee. You will be amazed how easily the ball goes into the air. If you are swinging correctly, you should knock the tee over each time you swing.

MYTH #4 - KEEP YOUR LEFT ARM STRAIGHT

During the backswing, you should keep your left arm *relatively* straight and fold your right arm. After the point of impact, your left arm folds and your right arm straightens, just the opposite as in the backswing. Many golfers believe you should control the golf swing by keeping your left arm straight throughout the swing. However, if you keep your left arm straight after impact, the clubface will be open and the shot will always curve to the right. To avoid this problem, do not try to keep your left arm perfectly straight in the backswing. It may bend slightly.

WOODS VS. IRONS

The golf swing is basically the same with your woods or irons. However, there are a couple of adjustments you will need to make. First, at address, the ball is placed more toward your left foot with your woods than your irons. Next, the swing resembles a sweeping motion with the woods. With the irons, you will feel like you are hitting down through the shot more than with a wood. As a result, you will often take a divot when hitting the ball with irons, but should not with your woods.

When using woods, beginners often ask how high to tee up the ball on their tee shot. As shown in figure 9.19, half of the ball should be above the top of your clubhead to help get the club under the ball.

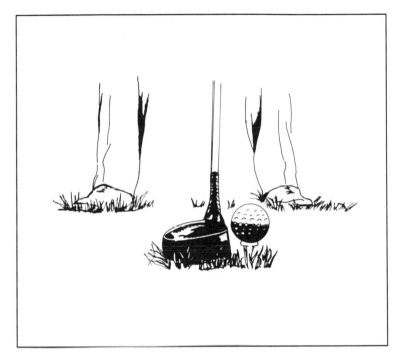

[Figure 9.19]
Proper Height to Tee Up the Golf Ball

UNEVEN LIES

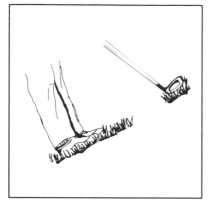

[Figure 9.20]
Ball Above Your Feet

When the ball is above your feet, your tendency will be to hit the ground before the ball, or hit the shot left of your target. This is called a *pull, draw,* or *hook shot.* Adjustments: 1) Aim right of your target. 2) Grip the club farther down the shaft, so that you do not hit the ground during the swing. 3) Use a club one number lower than you would normally use, and swing easier. For example, if you would normally use a 5-iron, use a 4-iron instead.

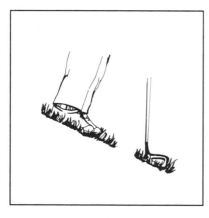

[Figure 9.21]
Ball Below Your Feet

When the ball is below your feet, the tendency will be to hit the top of the ball or hit the shot right of your target. This is called a *push, fade* or *slice shot.* Adjustments: 1) Aim left of your target. 2) Keep your weight more on the heels at address, because your body will tend to move forward toward the ball as you swing. 3) Make sure your body stays down during the shot. 4) Use a club one number lower than you would normally use and swing easier.

When hitting the ball from an uphill lie, the tendency is to hit the ball higher, shorter, and slightly to the left. Adjustments: 1) Aim right of your target. 2) Position the ball farther left of center than usual in your stance. 3) Level your shoulders to the slope of the hill at address. 4) Use a club one lower than you normally would.

[Figure 9.22]
Uphill Lie

When hitting the ball from a downhill lie, the tendency is to hit the ball low and right of your target. Adjustments: 1) Aim to the left of your target. 2) Position the ball right and back of center in your stance. 3) Level your shoulders to the slope of the hill.

[Figure 9.23]
Downhill Lie

1

2

3

4

[Figure 9.24]
The Full Swing
(Grid background furnished by Jason Jecks)

5

6

7

8

10

THE SHORT GAME - PUTTING

ABOUT THE SHORT GAME

The game of golf is unlike most other sports because there are so many different facets to the game. In the previous chapter we discussed the full-swing. During the next two chapters we will discuss a variety of golf shots. The game of golf is often divided into two different categories, the *long game* and the *short game*. The long game includes the full-swing for the woods and irons. The short game includes all the shots on the green and within approximately 90 yards of the green including: *putting, chipping, pitching, bunker play* and *half shots*.

The short game shots are your scoring shots. During a round of golf a skilled golfer often misses the green in *regulation*, while the average golfer rarely hits the green in regulation. Par less two is the number of shots you have to get onto the green in regulation. It is possible for someone to consistently shoot lower scores than his or her opponent by having a better short game, even though the opponent can hit the ball much farther. Good short game shots allow you to take advantage of your good shots, and also gives you the opportunity to make up for poor shots.

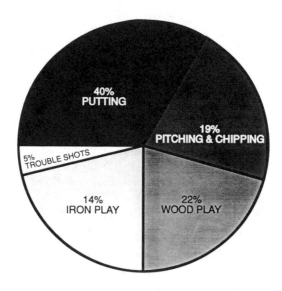

[Figure 10.1]
Percentage of Shots Taken

Figure 10.1 shows the percentage of each type of shot taken during a round of golf for an average golfer that shoots between 80 to 100, for 18 holes. You will notice that putting accounts for 40 percent of shots taken and the remainder of the short game shots account for 19 percent. Therefore, 59 percent of your shots are played on or near the green. It only makes sense that *the time you spend practicing each shot should be proportional to how often you will use the shot on the golf course.* Still, most golfers spend the majority of their time hitting balls on the driving range, while neglecting their short game. As a result, they never get their golf scores as low as they could.

Regardless of age, strength, or gender, all golfers have the ability to become skilled at the short game. The shots for the short game do not take strength, because all the shots are on or close to the green. To excel in the short game, you need knowledge, along with time to practice the different shots regularly.

The short game will cover two separate chapters. We will start with putting in this chapter, then cover the other short game shots in the next chapter. There is no clear guide to determine exactly what type of shot to use when near the green. When deciding what type of shot to use near the green, try to putt whenever possible. If you cannot putt, then use the chip shot, and if neither of these shots will work, then use the pitch shot.

PUTTING

As mentioned earlier, approximately 40 percent of all the shots played during a round of golf are putts. Therefore, adequate time should be spent learning the fundamentals of putting. The putting stroke is the most accurate shot, because it is the simplest of all the shots. The putting stroke is used primarily when you are on the putting green. If you are on the *fringe* or close to the green and the area between the ball and the green is smooth, then you may also want to putt the ball. If the area is not smooth, then you should use a chip or pitch shot.

METHODS OF PUTTING

Figure 10.2 shows the two different methods of putting. Both methods produce a simple pendulum-like motion. The *traditional* putting stroke is the most common method of putting. The *side-saddle* putting stroke is becoming increasingly popular for some golfers, especially seniors, to minimize back stress. As a beginner, first try the traditional method of putting. If you do not become comfortable with this method, then you may want to consider the side-saddle putting stroke. A longer putter is required for the side-saddle putting stroke.

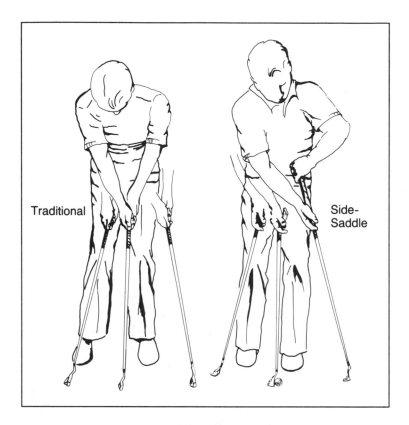

[Figure 10.2]
Methods of Putting

THE FUNDAMENTALS OF PUTTING

The pre-swing fundamentals of putting are similar to the pre-swing fundamentals of the full-swing. Your posture and alignment are the same. The ball position should be between the center of your feet and the inside edge of your left foot, so you strike the ball on the up-swing portion of the pendulum.

The most common putting grip used is the *reverse-overlapping grip*. Figure 10.3. Both the overlapping grip and the 10-finger grip discussed in Chapter 4 are also used when putting. The interlocking grip however is rarely used for putting. Test the various grips and use whatever grip feels most comfortable. When gripping the putter, you should have your thumbs go down the center of the shaft, which is different from the grip for the full-swing. Also, make sure you grip the club loosely, to help improve your *feel*.

[Figure 10.3]
Reverse-Overlapping Putting Grip

For successful putting you need to control only two variables: the distance and direction of the putt. Listed below are five easy-to-follow swing fundamentals to help you control the distance and direction of your putts.

Fundamental #1 - Develop A Consistent Swing Path

To develop the feel of the proper path of the putting stroke, simply practice putting in-between two clubs or two 2" x 4"s. It is best to practice this drill with short putts of 15 feet or less. Figure 10.4.

[Figure 104]
Putting Drill

Fundamental #2 - Keep The Clubhead Square To Your Path

Like the first fundamental, keeping the clubhead square to your path will also promote consistent direction. The longer you can keep the putter face square, or perpendicular to your target line, the better your chance of hitting your putt along the line. Figure 10.5.

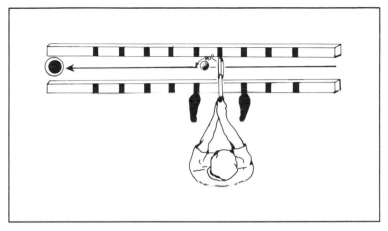

[Figure 10.5]
Keep the Putter Head Square (Perpendicular) to the Target Line

Fundamental #3 - Keep Your Lower Body Stationary

When hitting a wood or iron in the full-swing, you are trying to advance the ball a great distance. Therefore, it is necessary to transfer your weight throughout the swing. When putting, you only need to roll the ball a short distance. The less movement from your body, the more consistent and accurate you will be. Keep your lower body stationary during the entire putting stroke. You should keep your weight evenly distributed on both feet. Your knees should also maintain the same flex throughout the stroke. To help see if your lower body moves during your putting stroke, practice your putting stroke in front of the mirror.

Fundamental #4 - Do Not Bend Your Wrist When Putting

A common error for beginning golfers is that they overuse their hands and wrists when putting. The muscles in your hands can do many delicate tasks; however overuse of your hands can also destroy the putting stroke. As shown in figure 10.6, the relationship between your hands, arms and the putter should remain the same throughout the putting stroke. Your shoulders, arms and hands should all move together as one unit. To achieve this, you should feel as if the putting stroke is controlled with your shoulders and arms, not your hands and wrists.

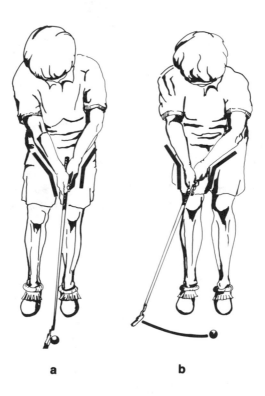

a   b

[Figure 10.6]
The Putting Stroke

Fundamental #5 - Accelerate Through Impact

During the forward movement of the putting stroke accelerate the club through the point of impact and continue toward your target. For example: As shown in figure 10.2, if you go 6 inches back on your backswing, then you should go at least 6 inches past the ball on your follow-through. Figure 10.7 shows a good drill to eliminate a long backswing and promote a good follow-through. For this drill, line up a few balls along the same target line. Place them approximately 6 to 8 inches apart. Starting with the ball that is closest to the hole, putt each one in order, using your right hand only. Make sure that you do not hit the

c

d

The relationship between the club and the wrist remain the same throughout the putting stroke.

next ball back on your backswing. Remember, you should always follow through at least the same distance as your backswing.

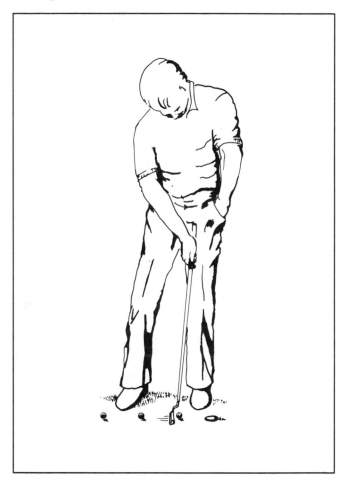

[Figure 10.7]
Putting Drill

READING THE GREEN

Greens are rarely flat. Therefore, once you learn the fundamentals of the putting stroke, you will find an important element to successful putting will be learning to *read* the green. Reading the green means determining the *speed* needed and how much the ball will curve, or *break*, when putted. The speed and *slope* of greens will vary at each course and even with the time of day. When playing, it is always helpful to watch others putt to see how the ball curves. Both practice and experience are necessary to learn how to read greens.

To align yourself for a putt that will curve, figure out how much you think the putt will curve, and make that your imaginary target. For example, if you think a putt is going to break approximately 1 foot from left to right, then your imaginary hole would be 1 foot to the left of the hole, and you should adjust your alignment, as shown in figure 10.8.

LONG PUTTS

The game is designed to allow two putts, or strokes per green. If your approach shot to the green lands close to the hole, then you will sometimes use only one putt to get the ball in the hole. If your approach shot lands farther from the hole, then your goal should be to get the ball into the cup in two putts. To help get your first putt close to the hole, imagine a 3 foot circle around the hole and try to roll the ball within that circle. Furthermore, always get your putts to the hole or past the hole. A putt that is short of the hole never has a chance to go in, even if it is on the correct target line. Figure 10.8.

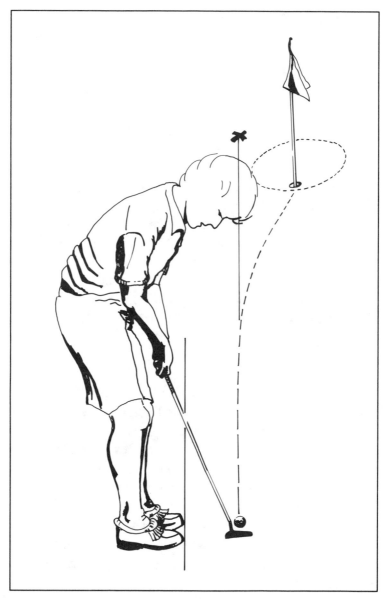

[Figure 10.8]
Alignment for a Putt That Breaks from Left to Right

[Figure 10.9]
The Putting Stroke

11

THE SHORT GAME - CHIPPING, PITCHING, BUNKER PLAY AND HALF TO THREE-QUARTER SHOTS

In this chapter we will discuss the remaining short game shots: the *chip shot, pitch shot, bunker shot* and *half to three-quarter shot.* Each of these shots are used when you are within approximately 90 yards of the hole. First, we will start with the shots used closest to the green and then move back away from the green.

CHIP SHOT VS. PITCH SHOT

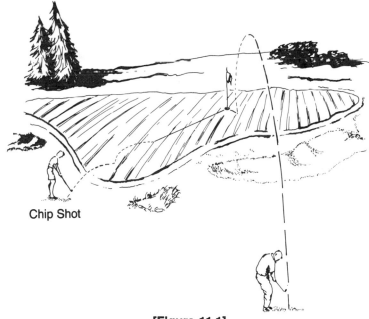

Chip Shot

Pitch Shot

[Figure 11.1]
Chip Shot vs. Pitch Shot

When you are within approximately 50 yards of the hole, you may use either a chip shot or pitch shot to get the ball onto the green. Figure 11.1. The chip shot is in the air for a short period of time and rolls most of the time. The pitch shot is in the air most of the time and rolls less. To select which shot you should hit, determine: 1) Can you roll the ball most of the way to the hole, or 2) Do you need to fly the ball most of the way to the hole? How far you are from the green and how far the hole is from the edge of the green will determine which shot to use. Whenever possible, it is best to roll the ball, since the more the ball is in the air, the more difficult it is to control the distance the shot will travel. Regardless of which type of shot you use, the ball should usually land on the green first, then roll to the hole. Try not to let the ball land short of the green and then bounce up onto the green.

THE CHIP SHOT

An important factor for the chip shot is club selection. Many golfers use just their 7-iron or pitching wedge for chipping, however, this is not recommended. When chipping you will be using irons ranging from the 7-, 8-, 9-irons, pitching wedge, and the sand wedge. You should not use below a 7-iron, because it becomes difficult to control the distance of your shot with a 6-iron or less. When chipping, use the same swing with each club and let the difference in the loft of the club determine the distance the ball will go. Figure 11.2.

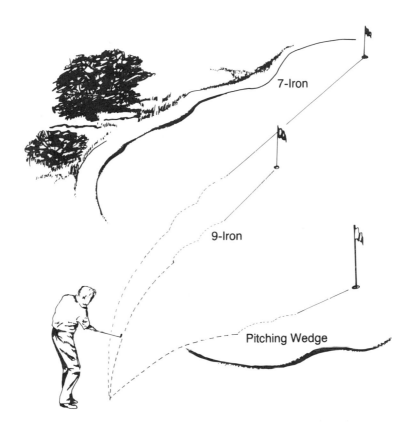

[Figure 11.2]
The Chip Shot

FUNDAMENTALS OF THE CHIP SHOT

a   b

[Figure 11.3]
The Chip Shot

As shown in figure 11.3, the chip shot is basically a putt, with four adjustments made to your setup. These adjustments include:

STANCE

Rather than aligning your feet parallel to your target, as in a square stance, your stance is open. This same stance should also be used for the other short game shots discussed in this chapter.

WEIGHT DISTRIBUTION

At address, your weight should be placed primarily on your left leg. You should have 70 percent of the weight on your left leg and 30 percent on your right leg. The distribution of your weight should not change during the chip shot.

d

c

GRIP

Grip down on the club, so your hands are just above where the grip ends and the shaft becomes visible. This is suggested for all shots around the green, to give you better feel and control of the club. Also, grip the club lightly to minimize tension.

BALL PLACEMENT

Place the ball in front of you. The ball should be placed closer to the inside of your right foot than the inside of your left foot.

Like a putt, the chip shot is a simple pendulum motion. During both shots, you do not use your wrist, so your hands, arms, shoulders and club work as a unit. Also, there is very little movement, if any, from your lower body which stays stationary throughout each shot. When chipping, the club you use has more loft than when putting, and this will automatically make the ball go in the air.

THE PITCH SHOT

Sometimes it is necessary to fly the ball over obstacles to get onto the green. This type of shot is called a *pitch shot.* Figure 11.4. The pitch shot may be used from farther off the green than the chip shot. The ball can go farther with this shot because you start to let your wrist break on the backswing, and the swing is longer. It is more difficult to execute the pitch shot than the chip shot, since you are breaking, or *cocking,* your wrist. A simple key to remembering the difference between the pitch and chip shot is: without using your wrist (the chip shot), the ball will fly lower and not travel as far; when using your wrist, (the pitch shot), the ball will fly higher and can travel farther.

[Figure 11.4]
The Pitch Shot

FUNDAMENTALS OF THE PITCH SHOT

The setup for the *pitch shot* is the same as for the chip shot, except the ball should be placed in front of you, and centered between your feet. As with the chip shot, your stance should be narrow and open to your target, the weight favors your left leg, and you grip down on the club.

Club selection is different for the pitch shot. For a pitch shot, you should use one of the three wedges discussed in Chapter 3 (pitching, middle or sand wedge) to help loft the ball into the air. As shown in figure 11.4, the length of the swing will determine how far you hit the ball. Your weight transfer should be subtle, and based on the length of your swing. Imagine throwing a ball under-handed as illustrated in figure 11.5. As you need to throw the ball farther, your arm swing and weight transfer will gradually increase. This is the same feeling you experience when hitting a pitch shot.

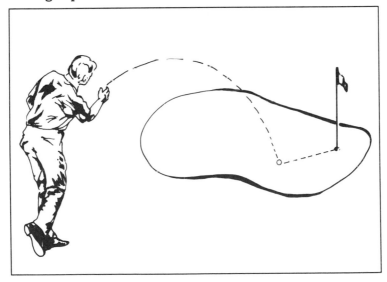

[Figure 11.5]
The pitch shot is similar to throwing the ball under-hand.

A common error with the pitch shot is that the hands become too active during the forward swing, which minimizes consistency. You should not try to help the ball up with your hands. The club will have plenty of loft. When swinging, focus on hitting the ball and the grass at the same time. The ball will automatically go into the air. To help get below the ball, take practice swings along the grass. When taking these swings you should hear the club swish through the grass. If you do not hear anything, that means you would have missed or hit the top of the golf ball.

Figure 11.6 shows a proper *finish*. Notice the position of the clubhead at the finish position. The toe is not pointing straight up to the sky like on a normal shot. The toe is pointing to the horizon. This keeps the clubface open, giving the ball a higher flight and softer landing. It is very important to take a close look at figure 11.6. Practice this shot in front of a mirror to assure you are in the correct finish position. When in this position, you should feel your right arm underneath or closer to the ground than your left arm.

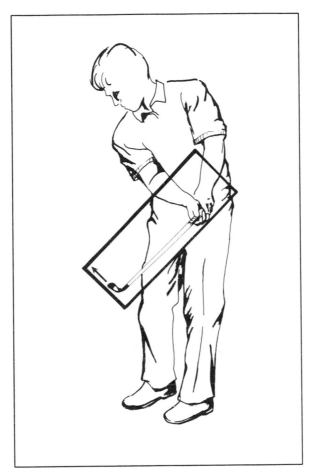

[Figure 11.6]
A Proper Finish to the Pitch Shot

THE HALF TO THREE-QUARTER SHOT

Both the chip and pitch shots limit the distance you can hit the ball. As you get farther from the green you will need to apply a few different fundamentals. Remember, there is little or no weight transfer in the pitch or chip shots, which restrict the distance the ball will travel. If you try to use the chip or pitch shot from too far off the green, you will lose your balance and rhythm. This indicates that you should use a *half to three-quarter shot.* Figure 11.7. This shot may be used from approximately 40 to 90 yards from the green.

Fundamentals of the Half To Three-Quarter Shot

The half to three-quarter shot should resemble the half-swing drill. At address, your stance should be open and

a

[Figure 11.7]
The Half to Three-quarter Shot

more narrow than for a full-swing. Your weight should be evenly distributed between your feet. The farther you need to hit the shot, the longer your arm swing will be. As the length of your swing increases, so will your weight transfer. Last, notice the position of the club in the finish position. Figure 11.7. The toe is pointing straight to the sky. *The difference between the half to three-quarter shot and the pitch shot is the follow-through and finish position.*

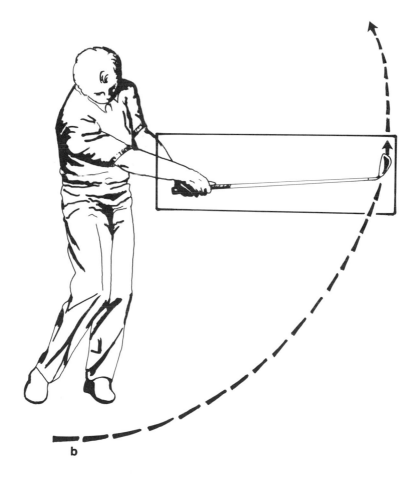

b

BUNKER SHOTS

Most golfers dread the thought of having to hit their ball out of the *bunker*. Playing from the sand is not easy for most players simply because they do not understand the fundamentals needed for playing bunker shots.

There are two types of bunker shots, the *greenside bunker* shot and the *fairway bunker* shot. The greenside bunker shot is the only shot in golf where the club does not hit the ball. The club first enters the sand, then, as the club moves through the sand the displacement of the sand pops the ball up into the air. Figure 11.8.

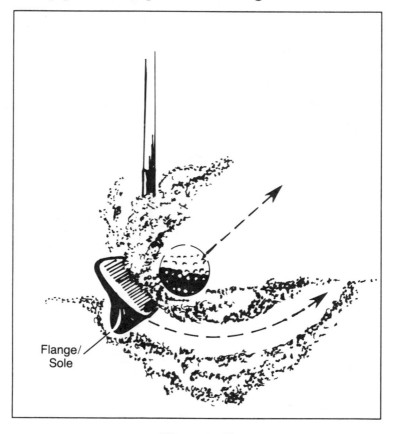

Flange/
Sole

[Figure 11.8]
The Bunker Shot

It is important to use the correct type of club in the sand. A sand wedge is much more effective in the sand than other wedges because the sand wedge has: 1) a larger sole or flange to keep the club from digging too much, 2) more loft to lift the ball, and 3) more weight in the head of the golf club to help keep the club moving through the sand.

The Flange

The first step in understanding proper sand technique is to understand the purpose of the *flange* of the sand wedge. Figure 11.8. The flange is the rounded *sole* or bottom of the club. The flange is designed to minimize the depth the clubhead will go into the sand. At address, the face of the sand wedge should be in an open position, so the flange will enter the sand before the leading edge. Figure 11.9. When you open the clubface, the club will make a shallow path, or *bounce,* as it goes through the sand. If you set the face square to your target, the leading edge will enter the sand first. As a result, the clubhead will dig deeper into the sand, slowing the club and leaving the ball in the bunker. If the ball is buried in the sand, you will need the club to go deeper into the sand to get the ball in the air, so square the face of the club.

To better understand the purpose of the flange, imagine putting a spoon in the sand. If the rounded bottom of the spoon hits the sand first, the spoon would not go into the sand. If the spoon is turned on its side, it would easily dig into the sand.

Fundamentals For The Greenside Bunker Shot

For the greenside bunker shot the setup and the swing are basically the same as the pitch shot. You should, however, consider a couple of changes when setting up. First, make sure you have secure footing. If the sand is soft, make sure you dig your feet in the sand to get a good base or foundation. Second, make sure you hold the club closer to where the grip meets the shaft, since your feet will be lower in the sand. Otherwise, the club will dig too far into the sand during the swing. Last, open the clubface unless the ball is buried in the sand. Figure 11.9.

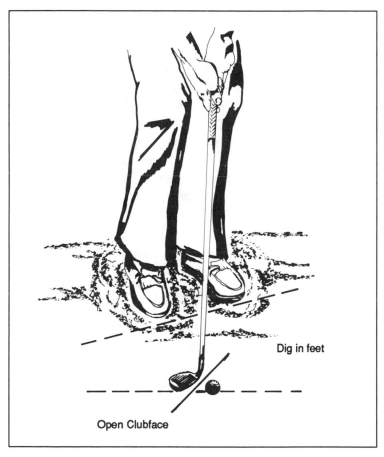

[Figure 11.9]
Address Position for a Bunker Shot

For the greenside bunker shot, there are two important swing thoughts. First, you must *swing aggressively*, because the weight of the sand greatly reduces clubhead speed. When preparing for this shot, visualize hitting the shot five times farther than you actually need to.

The second swing thought is make sure you *hit the sand*. Figure 11.10. As mentioned earlier, your club does not make contact with the ball for this type of shot. While swinging, forget about the ball and think about the sand. Your club should enter the sand between 3 to 4 inches behind the ball. If you try to enter the sand too close to the ball, you are likely to take too little sand and send the ball sailing over the green. Do not pick an exact spot behind the ball that you want to hit, simply pick out a general area and your swing will adjust.

Both swing thoughts, to swing aggressively and to hit the sand, must be followed for a successful sand shot. For instance, if you swing aggressively without taking any sand, the ball will either go way past your target or you will hit the top of the ball. If you take sand and do not swing aggressively, the weight of the sand will slow down the club to the point the ball will not go far enough to get out of the bunker.

The last shot we will discuss in this chapter is the fairway bunker shot. This shot is not considered part of the short game, however, since we are currently discussing bunker play, we will review the fairway bunker shot.

[Figure 11.10]
A Greenside Bunker Shot

Fundamentals For The Fairway Bunker Shot

A fairway bunker shot is just like any other normal full-swing, except the shot takes place in the sand rather than on the grass. The trajectory necessary for your ball to get over the lip, or edge, of the bunker is a primary factor in determining club selection for bunker shots.

It can be difficult to maintain proper footing in the bunker, which makes this shot harder than a regular full-swing shot. To improve your footing during the swing, address the ball by working your feet into the sand and brace your right foot on an angle as shown in figure 11.11.

Do not hit the sand before striking the ball, for this will reduce the distance the ball will travel. Last, the ball normally will not go as far when you are hitting a shot from within the sand. To adjust, use a club one number lower than you normally would from that distance.

[Figure 11.11]
Right Foot Position for a Fairway Bunker Shot

[Figure 11.12]
The Chip Shot

[Figure 11.13]
The Pitch Shot

[Figure 11.14]
The Half to Three-quarter Shot

Putting Stroke

Chip Shot

Pitch Shot

Half to Three Qrtr. Shot

[Figure 11.15]

12

PLAYING THE GAME OF GOLF

We have covered a number of topics concerning the game of golf. Now it is time to get started on the golf course. For many, golf is more difficult to learn and understand than other sports. The game does take some time to learn, however, don't let this discourage you. Part of the enjoyment of playing golf is experiencing the satisfaction of improvement as you play and practice. *Furthermore, with a proper introduction to the game, golf is easier to learn.*

To ease your introduction into the game, there are a number of items to consider. Begin playing golf on a golf course as soon as possible. The sooner you get on the golf course, the quicker you will learn about the game. As a beginner, it is best to play with a friend or family member that is an experienced golfer. They will be able to answer many of your questions, and help you around the golf course your first few times. The game can be played with one to four players in a group. Two players in a group are called a *twosome,* three players a *threesome,* and four players a *foursome.*

TYPES OF GOLF COURSES

There are different types of golf courses you may play; *par-3, executive, regulation,* and *championship.* Par-3 golf courses are the best courses when starting, because they are the shortest course, with each hole being a par-3. An executive course is also a good course to start on. This type of course is longer than a par-3, but shorter than a regulation course. Regulation courses are the most common courses. These courses are longer and more challenging than executive courses. Some of the more difficult regulation courses are called championship courses.

As mentioned, the length and difficulty of each course varies. Therefore, find out before you get to the course how difficult it is. You can determine the difficulty of most courses by getting either the *course rating* or the *slope rating*. The course rating compares the difficulty of the course to par. The rating is determined primarily on the length of the golf course, with little emphasis on the actual difficulty of the course. The slope rating rates the course on ten different variables. Therefore, the slope rating is a better indicator of the overall difficulty of a course.

A slope rating can range from 55 to 155. The average regulation course has a slope rating of 113. The majority of regulation courses have a slope rating between 100 and 120. Both the course and slope rating may vary based on the location of the tees. If you start playing on a regulation course, it is best to start on a course with a slope rating of 115 or less. Figure 12.1 shows a guide to the difficulty of a course based on the course and slope rating.

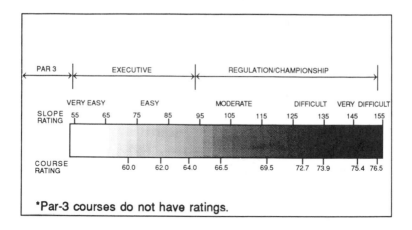

[Figure 12.1]

Course Rating/Slope Rating

(Information provided by the Golf Association of Michigan & Handicomp, Inc.)

MAKING A GOLF RESERVATION

Before going to a golf course, it is best to call to reserve a time to play, referred to as a *tee time*. The reservation policy for each course is different. Also check the following items:

1. Is the reservation for 9 or 18 holes?
2. What are peak times, and off-peak times to play? Play at off-peak times when beginning so you do not feel as rushed when playing.
3. If you will be paired up to play with other golfers not in your group? Many golf courses require that golfers play in groups of four, and will pair you with other golfers.
4. If you have the option to walk or do you have to take a cart?
5. If there is a dress code at the course?
6. If there is a minimum age requirement to bring children onto the course?
7. If rental clubs are available?

WHEN YOU GET TO THE COURSE

When arriving at the course, it is best to first check in at the golf shop. Most courses offer a *practice green* for you to warm up on before your round, and some courses also offer a *driving range.*

Before playing, always take a few minutes to stretch and loosen up. As with any sport, if you stretch your muscles before playing, you will be less likely to pull a muscle.

The first few times you play the game, if you are slowing up the golfers within your group or the groups behind you, then you do not need to play all of each hole. You may want to limit the number of strokes you take on each hole to nine. After six or seven shots, if your ball is not on the green yet, you may want to consider placing your ball on the front edge of the green. This will help you learn about the game without slowing up play. *Remember, you should be able to play each hole in 13 minutes or less.*

STARTING CHILDREN

When starting children in the game, make it fun and enjoyable. Depending on the age and ability of the child, you can let the children start each hole from either the forward tees, beginning of the fairway, or from within 150 yards from the green. To help them move along, you may let them play their shot from where you hit your shot.

13

PRACTICING EFFECTIVELY

Like the saying goes, practice makes perfect. Unlike other activities, practicing the game of golf is in itself enjoyable for many golfers. Many people spend more time practicing the game than actually playing.

To reach your potential, you must put adequate time into practicing each of the different types of golf shots. Golf does not require a lot of technical and analytical skill, as most people believe. The game requires that you learn a few basic fundamentals. To excel in golf, you must have the time, dedication, and discipline to learn how to do the fundamentals repetitively and consistently. Remember to *keep the swing as simple, free, and unrestricted as possible.*

All too often students receive a golf lesson, hit a few buckets of balls on the driving range, and then go back to their instructor frustrated. They believe there should be improvement in one or two hours. Remember, golf does take time to learn. Changing muscle memory takes time. Research indicates that if you want to change your muscle memory and transform the new muscle memory into a habit, you must work for two hours per day for approximately 30 consecutive days. Most people do not have that kind of time to dedicate to the game of golf. So, if you are making a change in your golf swing, develop a daily routine over a period of weeks or months to help make your changes a habit.

DEVELOPING A ROUTINE

To develop a consistent golf swing that works even under pressure, develop a *routine* when you are hitting each golf ball. Most golf professionals take the same amount of time to prepare and hit each shot, regardless of what is at stake for the shot. Too often a golfer will say, "All I need is a six on this hole and I will break 100 for the first time ever." Of course the golfer gets a score of 10 on the last hole, and does not make it. By developing a routine, you will minimize the effect tension has on your shot. To do this, start on the practice range, and prepare yourself to hit each shot the same way. Then make sure you follow this same procedure on the golf course, regardless of what shot you use.

When developing your routine, minimize the amount of time you stand still over the golf ball. Studies indicate that most professionals move their hands, feet, or head, until a split second before they swing. The longer you stand still over the golf ball, the harder it is to start the swing, and swing consistently. This is why batters in baseball wiggle their bat, and tennis players shuffle their feet while awaiting the serve. Golf is a game of motion and it is easier to create motion from motion, rather than from a static position.

SEQUENCE OF LEARNING

Before you focus too much attention on the fundamentals of swinging the club, first spend adequate time learning the correct pre-swing fundamentals - grip, posture, ball position, and alignment. These fundamentals directly affect the flight of the golf ball. Getting set up correctly to hit a golf shot is a major ingredient to developing consistant shot making.

AIM AT A TARGET WHEN PRACTICING

When practicing, the number one problem with golfers is that they do not select a specific target for each shot. When on a practice driving range, if you asked most golfers where they are aiming, they would say, "somewhere down the middle of the range." As a result, most golfers align their body to the target incorrectly, which develops problems in the swing itself. When practicing, always aim at a specific target. Lay down three clubs to help determine if you are aligned to your target correctly, and the ball is in the proper position. Figure 13.1. Also, *develop a visual image of your ball going to your target.* This will help to focus on where you would like the ball to go, rather than where you don't want the ball to go.

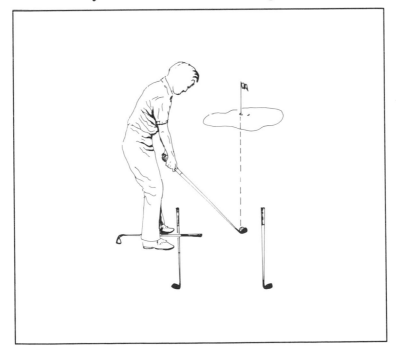

[Figure 13.1]
Alignment and Ball Position

14

WHAT TO CONSIDER WHEN BUYING YOUR GOLF CLUBS

Before purchasing any golf equipment, you should first play the game a few times. As a beginner, you want to make sure you enjoy the game and will continue to play in the future. Borrow a friend or family member's equipment, or rent a set from the course the first few times you play. Purchasing a set of golf clubs can be a major investment. It is important to become familiar with the game and how the equipment is used before making your investment.

Once you determine that you would like to purchase golf equipment, there are some items you should consider. First, there are several types of retailers that sell golf equipment, including on-course golf shops, off-course golf retailers, department stores, and mail-order companies. Golf equipment is also sold through the newspapers, magazines, bulletin boards, and word-of-mouth. As the buyer, only you can decide where you should purchase your equipment. The various sellers have different advantages and disadvantages, which you must consider. Regardless of where you get your golf clubs, there are some important principles to consider so that your clubs will best suit your size and ability.

When you are ready to purchase any golf equipment, you should first contact a knowledgeable golf professional or club-fitter in your area to discuss the following variables that will affect the golf equipment you need.

1. club length
2. lie angle
3. shaft flex
4. grip and grip size
5. swingweight & overall weight
6. clubhead design

CLUB LENGTH

When purchasing your woods, irons, or a putter, it is important to consider the *length* of the club. With such differences in the size and ability of different golfers, it is important to have clubs that are not too long or too short. Most clubs are made a *standard* length. There are differences in the standard lengths of men's, women's and children's clubs. Women's clubs are generally manufactured 1 inch shorter than men's clubs.

If you are taller or shorter than the average male or female, you should consider having the length of the shaft of your clubs longer or shorter than standard. Otherwise, you may experience additional difficulty when trying to swing the club. When purchasing a set of new clubs, if you need to have your clubs shorter or longer than standard, it is best to have the manufacturer make the change so that the weight, balance and feel of the club will be correctly adjusted. It may take a few extra days or weeks to receive specially ordered clubs, however, this wait will provide long-term benefits. Figure 14.1 illustrates how the length of a club can affect your posture.

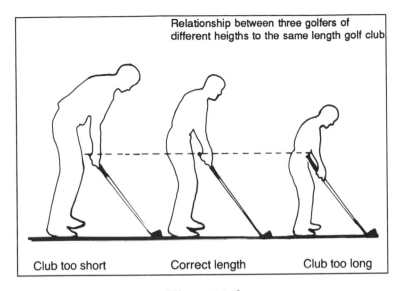

[Figure 14.1]
A tall male, short male, and child

LIE ANGLE

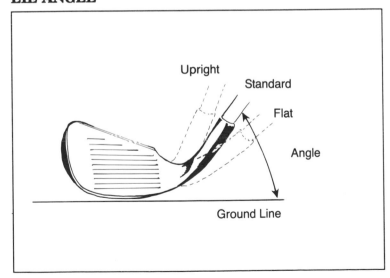

[Figure 14.2]
Different Lie Angles

The *lie* is the angle of the club shaft to the ground. Figure 14.2. A proper lie angle allows you to correctly set the clubhead on the ground, or sole the clubhead, when preparing to hit the golf ball. If your club is soled incorrectly, you will hit the ball off line as shown in figure 14.3.

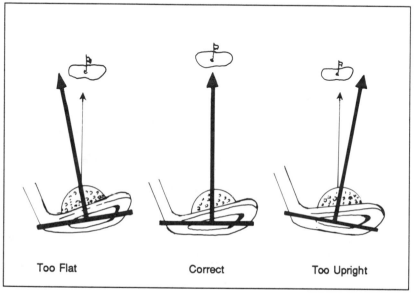

Too Flat   Correct   Too Upright

[Figure 14.3]
How the Lie Affects Shot Direction

Normally golf club manufacturers make irons in three different lies; *standard, flat,* and *upright.* A standard lie is designed to fit the average male or female. A flat lie helps the shorter golfers, and an upright lie helps taller golfers. Some woods are available in different lies, however, this is not as common.

Generally speaking, your height is the primary factor in determining whether you need a standard, flat, or upright lie. Figure 14.4. A club-fitting professional will also consider your arm length, athletic ability, strength, and body position at address when fitting you for clubs.

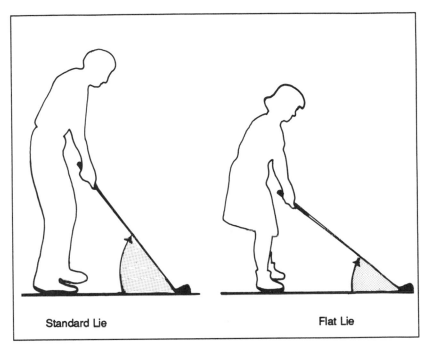

Standard Lie   Flat Lie

[Figure 14.4]
The Relationship Between the Height of a Golfer
and the Lie Angle of a Golf Club

SHAFT FLEX

During the golf swing, the shaft of the club bends or *flexes* to help provide additional clubhead speed. Figure 14.5. Golf clubs are designed with different *shaft flexes* for golfers of different strengths and athletic ability. A label directly below the grip shows the flexibility rating. Shafts are rated by numbers, letters, words, or abbreviations to describe the flexibility. For example, the words stiff (S), regular (R), or ladies' (L), are often used to describe the shaft flexes.

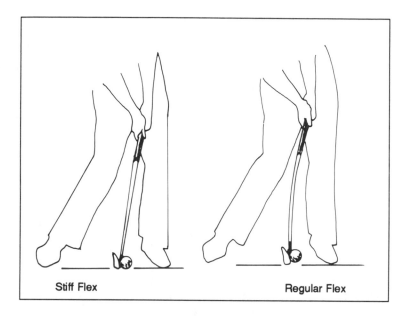

Stiff Flex   Regular Flex

[Figure 14.5]
Shaft Flex

Shafts are made of a number of different materials, including lightweight steel, graphite, titanium and boron. The type of shaft greatly affects the price of the golf club. Normally, the stronger the golfer, the stiffer the shaft should be. It is best to have a club-fitting professional see you swing in order to choose a flex that best suits your needs.

GRIP AND GRIP SIZE

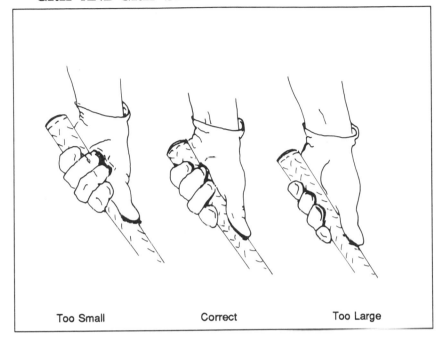

| Too Small | Correct | Too Large |

[Figure 14.6]
Grip Size

The grip is the handle on the golf club. Grips are made of various materials and textures: rubber, leather, etc. You may want to see a few different grips to decide which you like best. The grip also comes in different sizes to fit your hand size. It is important that it fit your hands properly, because the size of the grip directly affects your swing. The general rule is that the middle finger of your upper hand should just touch your palm. Figure 14.6.

SWINGWEIGHT AND OVERALL WEIGHT

The weight of a golf club can affect its performance. Normally, the proper weight for a club is built into the design. When fitting children, women, and senior golfers it is best to double-check to make sure the club is not too heavy.

There are two types of weights to consider with a club, *overall weight* and *swingweight*. The overall weight means exactly what it says. The swingweight measures how the club is balanced. Figure 14.7 shows how a club is measured for swingweight, along with the range of measurements. Each increment is approximately the weight of a dime.

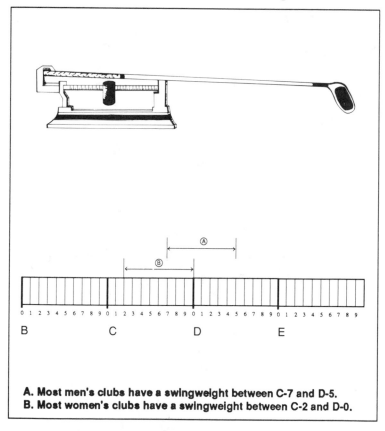

A. Most men's clubs have a swingweight between C-7 and D-5.
B. Most women's clubs have a swingweight between C-2 and D-0.

[Figure 14.7]
Swingweight Scale
(Information provided by J.C. Peterson, Indian Hills Golf Course, East Lansing, Michigan.)

CLUBHEAD DESIGN

Clubhead design is an important factor in club selection. An important factor in selecting any club is *"feel."* When purchasing clubs, try a few different types to determine which feels best to you. Try hitting balls with various clubs before you make your final purchase.

Irons

With irons, there are two distinct types, the *traditionally-designed* iron and the *perimeter-weighted* iron. Figure 14.8. Within each category, there is a wide variety of styles and designs to choose from.

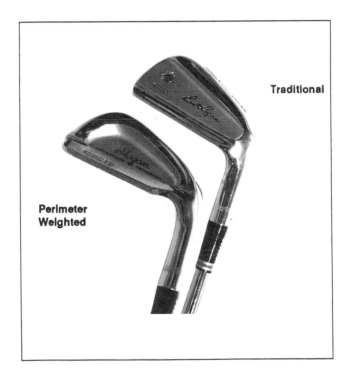

[Figure 14.8]
Traditional vs. Perimeter-Weighted Iron Heads

For most beginners, it is best to purchase perimeter-weighted irons, because it is easier to hit the golf ball more consistently with perimeter-weighted irons than with traditional irons. Traditional irons should be used by only the finest golfers, or for selected juniors, to help them develop a better golf swing. The primary difference between the two types of irons is the distribution of the weight in the club. A perimeter-weighted iron places the weight primarily around the lower portion of the clubhead, from the *heel* to the *toe*. Therefore, if you strike the ball on the heel or toe of the club, rather than the center, you will still have some force in your swing. This is why golfers say the perimeter-weighted club is more forgiving on poorly hit shots.

A traditional iron has most of the weight placed directly in the center of the clubface. Therefore, the clubs are very effective for the most skilled golfer, but not for the average or beginning golfer.

Woods

For woods, a major factor in club selection is the composition of the clubhead. Traditionally, wood clubheads were made of wood. Today, there are a number of other materials used to make woods, including metal and graphite. Wooden clubheads now make up a very small percentage of the new club market, while metal, graphite and other materials have become very popular.

Like perimeter-weighted irons, metal and graphite woods are more forgiving on poorly hit shots than wooden woods. Figure 14.9. Metal and graphite clubheads provide uniform weight distribution around the perimeter of the clubhead. It is difficult to control the overall weight distribution of a wooden clubhead because the density of each piece of wood varies. Metal and graphite woods are also more durable and require less maintenance than wooden woods.

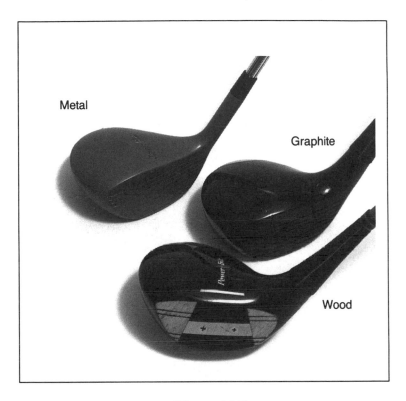

[Figure 14.9]
Wood, Metal and Graphite Woods

Putters

There are many different putters available to choose from. When selecting a putter, the primary concern is to select a putter that you feel comfortable with. Also, make sure the length and lie angle of the putter correctly fit your stance. Furthermore, it is helpful to select a putter that has a line on the top of the putter head indicating where to strike the ball.

FITTING JUNIORS

When starting children, care should be taken to assure that their clubs fit properly. Furnishing children with clubs that fit properly does not need to be expensive. Normally you can simply modify a set of existing clubs, or pick up some miscellaneous used clubs from an area golf course. It is best to contact a local golf professional or club-fitting professional to get your children started correctly, and make sure their equipment fits properly as they grow and improve. Figure 14.10 provides a helpful guide to fitting children based on their age and size.

Custom Fitting Table — Junior BOYS by Age, Average Height and Average Weight

Boy's Age	Boy's Avg. Height	Boy's Avg. Weight	Driving Wood				#5 Iron		Putter		Recommended Set Make-up	Shaft Flex Equivalent
			Avg. Length	Length Range	Loft	Weight Range	Avg Length	Length Range	Avg. Length	Length Range		
5	(3'8")	37 lbs	31"	30"-32"	5 wood 23°	12 to 12 1/2 oz. Total Weight	27"	26"-28"	25"	24"-26"	5 wood, 5,9 irons & P	L (Ladies)
6	(3'10")	41 lbs	31"	30"-32"	5 wood 23°	12 to12 1/2 oz. Total weight	27"	26"-28"	25"	24"-26"	5 wood, 5,9 irons & P	L (Ladies)
7	(4')	47 lbs	31"	30"-32"	5 wood 23°	12 to 12 1/2 oz. Total weight	27"	26"-28"	25"	24"-26"	5 wood, 5,9 irons & P	L (Ladies)
8	(4'1")	53 lbs	35"	32 1/2"-37"	4 wood 20°	11 1/2 to 12 oz. Total weight	30 1/2"	28 1/2"-32"	28 1/2"	26 1/2"-30"	4 wood, 5,7,9 irons & P	L (Ladies)
9	(4'3")	60 lbs	35"	32 1/2"-37"	4 wood 20°	11 1/2 to 12 oz. Total weight	30 1/2"	28 1/2"-32"	28 1/2"	26 1/2"-30"	4 wood, 5,7,9 irons & P	L (Ladies)
10	(4'5")	67 lbs	35"	32 1/2"-37"	4 wood 20°	11 1/2 to 12 oz. Total weight	30 1/2"	28 1/2"-32"	28 1/2"	26 1/2"-30"	4 wood, 5,7,9 irons & P	L (Ladies)
11	(4'7")	73 lbs	39"	38"-40 1/2"	3 wood 17°	11 to 11 1/2 oz. Total weight	33 1/2"	32 1/2"-34 1/2"	31 1/2"	30 1/2"-32"	3,5,7,9 irons & P 3,5 woods	L (Ladies)
12	(4'9 1/2")	83 lbs	39"	38"-40 1/2"	3 wood 17°	11 to 11 1/2 oz. Total weight	33 1/2"	32 1/2"-34 1/2"	31 1/2"	30 1/2"-32"	3,5,7,9 irons & P 3,5 woods	L (Ladies)
13	(5')	94 lbs	39"	38"-40 1/2"	3 wood 17°	11 to 11 1/2 oz. Total weight	33 1/2"	32 1/2"-34 1/2"	31 1/2"	30 1/2"-32"	3,5,7,9 irons & P 3,5 woods	L (Ladies or Flexible)
14	(5'3 1/4")	109 lbs	41 1/2"	40"-42"	2 wood 14°	C-8 to D-0 Swingweight	36"	35"-36 1/2"	34"	32 1/2"-34"	3-9 irons, PW, SW &P 2, 4, 5 woods	A (Flexible)
15	(5'5 3/4")	124 lbs	41 1/2"	40"-42"	2 wood 14°	C-8 to D-0 Swingweight	36"	35"-36 1/2"	34"	32 1/2"-34"	3-9 irons, PW, SW &P 2, 4, 5 woods	A (Flexible)
16	(5'7 3/4")	134 lbs	41 1/2"	40"-42"	2 wood 14°	C-8 to D-0 Swingweight	36"	35"-36 1/2"	34"	32 1/2"-34"	3-9 irons, PW, SW &P 2, 4, 5 woods	A (Flexible)
17	(5'9")	142 lbs	43"	42 1/2"-43 1/2"	Driver 12°	C-9 to D-3 Swingweight	37"	36 1/2"-37 1/2"	35"	34"-36"	1, 3, 4, 5 woods 3-9 irons, PW, SW & P	R or S (Med or Stiff)
18	(5'10")	149 lbs	43"	42 1/2"-43 1/2"	Driver 12°	C-9 to D-3 Swingweight	37"	36 1/2"-37 1/2"	35"	34"-36"	1, 3, 4, 5 woods 3-9 irons, PW, SW & P	R or S (Med or Stiff)

Junior clubfitting charts reprinted from Ralph Maltby's book, Golf Club Design, Fitting, Alteration & Repair, Golfworks, Newark, Ohio.

[Figure 14.10]

Fitting Juniors

Custom Fitting Table — Junior GIRLS by Age, Average Height and Average Weight

Girl's Age	Girl's Avg. Height	Girls Avg. Weight	Driving Wood Avg. Length	Length Range	Loft	Weight Range	#5 Iron Avg Length	Length Range	Putter Avg. Length	Length Range	Recommended Set Make-up	Shaft Flex Equivalent
5	43 1/2" (3'7 1/2")	37 lbs	31"	30"-32"	5 wood 23°	12 to 12 1/2 oz. Total Weight	27"	26"-28"	25"	24"-26"	5 wood, 5,9 irons & P	L (Ladies)
6	45 1/2" (3'9 1/2")	41 lbs	31"	30"-32"	5 wood 23°	12 to12 1/2 oz. Total Weight	27"	26"-28"	25"	24"-26"	5 wood, 5,9 irons & P	L (Ladies)
7	47 1/2" (3'11 1/2")	48 lbs	31"	30"-32"	5 wood 23°	12 to 12 1/2 oz. Total weight	27"	26"-28"	25"	24"-26"	5 wood, 5, 9 irons & P	L (Ladies)
8	48 1/2" (4'1/2")	52 lbs	35"	32 1/2"-37"	4 wood 20°	11 1/2 to 12 oz. Total weight	30 1/2"	28 1/2"-32"	28 1/2"	26 1/2"-30"	4 wood, 5, 9 irons & P	L (Ladies)
9	50 3/4" (4'2 3/4")	61 lbs	35"	32 1/2"-37"	4 wood 20°	11 1/2 to 12 oz. Total weight	30 1/2"	28 1/2"-32"	28 1/2"	26 1/2"-30"	4 wood, 5, 7, 9 irons & P	L (Ladies)
10	53" (4'5")	69 lbs	35"	32 1/2"-37"	4 wood 20°	11 1/2 to 12 oz. Total weight	30 1/2"	28 1/2"-32"	28 1/2"	26 1/2"-30"	4 wood, 5, 7, 9 irons & P	L (Ladies)
11	55 3/4" (4'7 3/4")	77 lbs	39"	38"-40 1/2"	3 wood 17°	11 to 11 1/2 oz. Total weight	33 1/2"	32 1/2"-34 1/2"	31 1/2"	30 1/2"-32"	3, 5, 7, 9 irons & P 3, 5 woods	L (Ladies)
12	58" (4'10")	87 lbs	39"	38"-40 1/2"	3 wood 17°	11 to 11 1/2 oz. Total weight	33 1/2"	32 1/2"-34 1/2"	31 1/2"	30 1/2"-32"	3, 5, 7, 9 irons & P 3, 5 woods	L (Ladies)
13	61" (5'1")	103 lbs	39"	38"-40 1/2"	3 wood 17°	11 to 11 1/2 oz. Total weight	33 1/2"	32 1/2"-34 1/2"	31 1/2"	30 1/2"-32"	3, 5, 7, 9 irons & P 3, 5 woods	L (Ladies or Flexible)
14	63" (5'3")	110 lbs	40"	39"-41"	2 wood 15°	C-2 to C-5 Swingweight	34 1/2"	34"-35"	32 1/2"	32"-33"	3-9 irons & P 2, 4, 7 woods	L (Ladies)
15	63 3/4" (5'3 3/4")	118 lbs	40"	39"-41"	2 wood 15°	C-2 to C-5 Swingweight	34 1/2"	34"-35"	32 1/2"	32"-33"	3-9 irons, PW, SW &P 2, 4, 7 woods	L (Ladies)
16	64" (5'4")	124 lbs	40"	39"-41"	2 wood 15°	C-2 to C-5 Swingweight	34 1/2"	34"-35"	32 1/2"	32"-33"	3-9 irons, PW, SW &P 2, 4, 7 woods	L (Ladies)
17	64" (5'4")	127	41 1/2"	41"-42 1/2"	Driver 13°	C-5 to C-9 Swingweight	35 1/2"	35"-36 1/2"	33 1/2"	33"-34 1/2"	3-9 irons, PW, SW &P 1, 3, 5, 7, 9 woods	L (Ladies)
18	64" (5'4")	127	41 1/2"	41"-42 1/2"	Driver 13°	C-5 to C-9 Swingweight	35 1/2"	35"-36 1/2"	33 1/2"	33"-34 1/2"	3-9 irons, PW, SW & P 1, 3, 5, 7, 9 woods	L (Ladies)

[Figure 14.10] Continued
Fitting Juniors

15

WHAT TO CONSIDER WHEN BUYING OTHER EQUIPMENT

GOLF BALLS

When learning to play golf, you should always use a ball with a durable cover so that the ball does not cut easily. Golf balls are manufactured with either a *two-* or *three-piece construction*. The two-piece golf ball, also called a solid ball, consists of a hard rubber inner core with a durable, hard to cut outer cover. A three-piece golf ball has a smaller, soft rubber inner core wrapped with rubber bands, then an outer cover. The composition of the outer cover affects the ball's durability. Surlyn is a material commonly used to make a durable outer cover. As you improve your golfing skills, you may want to use a ball with a softer cover, to give you better feel and control around the green. Balata is a material commonly used for a soft outer cover.

GOLF BAGS

Golf bags are used to carry golf clubs, golf balls and other miscellaneous equipment. They are available in various sizes, styles and materials. Remember when purchasing your bag, if you will be carrying or pulling your clubs around the golf course, get a lighter bag. A bag should last from three to five years, so the durability and construction are also important.

GOLF SHOES

As a beginner, it is not important to have golf shoes. Just use a pair of tennis shoes. If you do intend to continue playing the game, you should purchase a pair of golf shoes. Golf shoes will improve your footing, especially in wet playing conditions. Shoes are made from many different leather and synthetic materials, with a wide range in price. Comfort is important when buying golf shoes. If you walk 18 holes of golf, you are walking approximately 5 miles. Due to the amount of walking, durability is important. Some shoes are *guaranteed* to be *waterproof.* If you play in the morning when there is dew on the ground, or if you are playing during or after a rain, it is nice to keep your feet dry. The extra cost of waterproof shoes may be a good investment.

Golf shoes are available with spikes on the sole, which is the traditional type of golf shoe, or without spikes. Some golfers prefer the convenience of shoes without spikes. If you purchase shoes with spikes, before you use them it is best to remove all of the spikes, put a drop of lubricating oil in the fittings, then tightly secure the spikes. This is because manufacturers may not tightly secure the spikes.

GOLF GLOVES

A golf glove is an optional piece of golf equipment. Manufactured of leather or synthetic materials, gloves are designed to improve your grip on the club and minimize irritation to your hands. Normally a golf glove is worn on the hand closest to the target when addressing the ball. In other words, right-handed golfers wear the glove on the left hand and left-handed golfers wear the glove on the right hand. If your hands are extremely delicate or are easily irritated, you may want to wear a glove on both hands. To increase the life of a leather glove, lay the glove back in its package after use. This will help keep the glove from drying out and cracking.

PULL CARTS

Pull carts are used to help transport your clubs around the golf course. There are a number of pull carts on the market. When buying a pull cart, consider the overall weight, quality of construction, and how easily the pull cart folds up for transporting.

RAINWEAR

Rainwear is protective clothing worn when playing golf in inclement weather. When purchasing rainwear, it is best to choose rainwear that is guaranteed to be *waterproof.* Water resistant rainwear will not repel water in heavy rain.

UMBRELLAS

When purchasing an umbrella, choose one with a fiberglass handle so that it does not attract lightning. Durability is also important since the most common problem with umbrellas is that they break in heavy winds.

HEAD WEAR

With increasing concern about sunlight exposure, you may want to protect your head and face with proper head wear. If not, you should carry sunscreen in your golf bag so it is always available while playing.

BALL RETRIEVERS

With the increasing price of golf balls, many golfers purchase ball retrievers to help reach their golf balls if they land in water hazards. Remember, do not spend too long trying to retrieve your ball, for this may hold up other golfers.

CLOSING THOUGHTS

In closing, I would like to leave you with a special note. I have spent numerous hours working on a computer, and with the illustrator, Denny Arnett, to prepare this book. Certain parts of the text were very easy to write, while others were not. When putting the book together, for each step forward, there was a step backward. However, as I progressed with this challenging, yet enjoyable project, I realized one major thing. This book reflects the essence of the game of golf and life itself - *keep plugging along, work hard, and you will make progress.*

This text was not written to make you an expert golfer. It was written to bring enjoyment into your life through the game of golf. I hope in some way you will look back as you are playing the game and be thankful for the time you took to read this book. Most of all, I hope you learned as much reading it as I did writing it.

As you learn more about the game, this book should serve as a helpful reference guide. In addition, to maximize your golf abilities, I suggest you get professional instruction from a reputable golf professional in your area.

A STORY OF A CHAMPION

While attending college, I worked at a country club in Dallas, Texas. At that time, there was a young man named Brian Watts. He was 17 years old and eager to learn the game of golf. This young man played and practiced several hours each day. It was obvious that he had a love for the game. One night, while helping a student at a local driving range, I noticed Brian hitting balls at the far end of the range. It was cold that night, and getting late, but there he was practicing. The range at the country club was closed since it was dark, yet he was working to improve his game, even after a full day at the course.

Later that winter, we experienced exceptionally cold weather in December. There was a period of almost 30 days where the temperature did not reach freezing. Naturally, the play at the golf course came to a standstill, except every day after school, Brian practiced putting and chipping around the practice green.

Fortunately, he did have some natural ability. More importantly, Brian had dedication and discipline. Four years later, he shot one of the greatest rounds in the history of collegiate golf. With a last round score of 66 at the Ohio State Scarlet Golf Course, Brian led his team, Oklahoma State, to the 1987 NCAA Division I National Golf Championship. He also went on to become a two-time Collegiate All-American. Some people might say Brian plays so well because he has natural ability. Actually, he plays so well because he has *dedication, discipline,* and *a love for the game of golf!*

GOLF RELATED TERMS

ACE: Hitting the first shot from the tee into the hole, also referred to as a hole-in-one.

ADDRESSING THE BALL: The position a player takes in preparing to take a stroke.

APPROACH SHOT: A shot hit to the putting green.

APRON: The grass that borders the green, normally slightly higher than the grass on the green. Also referred to as the fringe.

AWAY: The player that is farthest from the hole.

BACK NINE OR BACK SIDE: The last nine holes of an 18-hole round, also called the in-nine.

BACK DOOR: When a ball rolls around the hole, and then falls into the hole from the back side of the hole.

BACKSPIN: Spin put on the ball that helps it stop after it lands. Increasing the loft of a club results in more backspin for a shot.

BENT GRASS: A fine textured grass used on the green and sometimes on the tees and fairways.

BEST BALL: A team competition using the best player's score on each hole. For instance on hole number one, if one player gets a five, and his or her partner gets a four, the best ball score for the team on the first hole would be a four.

BIRDIE: A score of one under par.

BITE: When a shot stops quickly due to the backspin on the ball.

BLIND SHOT: When the spot where you want to hit the ball is not visible when taking your shot.

BOGEY: A score of one over par.

BREAK OF GREEN: Hills, slopes or contours on the surface of a putting green that make the ball curve.

BUNKER: A hazard near the green or fairway that includes a depression or mounding in the landscape and is often filled with sand.

BURIED LIE: A ball imbedded in the sand, usually making the shot more difficult.

CADDIE: A person that carries a players golf equipment and helps with club selection and strategy of play.

CALLAWAY SYSTEM: A scoring method used to handicap players that do not have an established handicap. This type of scoring method is often used for one-day golf outings.

CARRY: The distance a ball must travel in the air before touching the ground.

CASUAL WATER: A temporary collection of water, not in a water hazard.

CHIP SHOT: A short, low shot to the green.

CHOKE DOWN: When the club is held closer to where the grip and the shaft meet.

CLOSED CLUBFACE: When your clubface is aligned left of your target.

CLUBFACE: The part of the club that hits the ball.

COURSE RATING: A rating system that assigns each course a number based on the difficulty of the golf course. The course rating is used to calculate a player's handicap and is made in comparison to par.

CUP: The hole in the putting green; 4 1/4 inches in diameter.

CUT SHOT: A shot that travels from right to left.

DIVOT: A piece of sod often taken when taking a stroke.

DOGLEG: A golf hole that curves left or right.

DORMIE: A situation in match play when a player or team is as many holes ahead as there are holes remaining to play.

DOUBLE BOGEY: A score of two over par on a hole.

DOUBLE EAGLE: A score of three under par on a hole.

DOWN: The number of holes or strokes a player is behind his or her opponent.

DRAW: A shot that curves slightly from the right to the left.

DRIVER: Another term for the 1-wood.

DUB: When a shot is poorly hit.

DUCK HOOK: A low shot that starts left of the target and goes further left.

DUFFER: A player with poor golf skills.

EAGLE: A score of two under par on a hole.

EMBEDDED BALL: A ball buried in soft ground.

FADE: A shot that curves slightly from the left to the right.

FAIRWAY: The closely mowed area of grass between the tee and the green.

FAT SHOT: When the club hits the ground before the ball, normally resulting in a poor shot.

FERAL: A plastic fitting where the clubhead meets the shaft.

FLAGSTICK OR FLAG: A tall, straight indicator with a flag attached to the top to help identify the location of the hole on the green. The movement of the flag also indicates how hard the wind is blowing.

FLANGE: The bottom or sole of the club.

FOLLOW-THROUGH: The part of the swing from the point of impact with the ball to the finish.

FORE!!: A universal word yelled when your shot goes toward another golfer.

FORECADDIE: A person assigned by a tournament committee to help spot where the golf balls land for players in a tournament.

FOURSOME: A group of four golfers playing a round of golf together.

FRIED EGG: A lie in the sand trap where the ball is imbedded in it's own impact mark.

FRONT NINE OR FRONT SIDE: The first nine holes in a round of golf.

GRAIN: The direction the grass grows or lies on the putting green. The grain can affect the amount a ball will break or curve when putting.

GREEN OR PUTTING GREEN: The closely-mowed surface where the hole, or cup, is located on which you putt.

GREENS FEE: The rate you pay to play a round of golf.

GRIP: The part of the shaft covered with rubber or leather where the club is held.

GROSS SCORE: The score a player has before his/her handicap is deducted.

GROUND UNDER REPAIR: A marked area of the course where work is being done.

GROUNDING THE CLUB: When the sole of the club touches the ground while addressing the ball.

HALVED OR HALVING A HOLE: A term used in match play when both players get the same score on a hole.

HANDICAP: A number representing a players ability in relation to par, used to equalize players with different abilities in a competition.

HAZARD: Any bunker or body of water on the golf course.

HEEL: The area of the clubhead near the neck or shaft of the club.

HEELED SHOT: When the club hits the ball near the heel of the club.

HOLE: A round receptacle 4 1/4 inches in diameter and at least 4 inches deep in the green. Also one unit of a golf course.

HOLE HIGH: A shot that lies even with the hole but to either side.

HOLE-OUT: To complete the play of a hole when the ball lands in the cup.

HONOR: The privilege of hitting first from the tee. Determined by the lowest score on the previous hole or coin toss for the first hole.

HOOK: A shot that curves from the right to the left.

HOSEL: The part of the clubhead where the shaft goes into the clubhead, also referred to as the neck.

INSERT: A piece of material in the face of a wood head, to improve the durability of the face from the impact between the ball and the club.

INSIDE-TO-OUTSIDE SWING PATH: This term is used in reference to the target line. The club is traveling left of the target line before impact and right of the target line after impact, normally resulting in a ball flight that starts to the right of your target.

LAG OR LAG PUTT: When a golfer tries to hit a long putt close to the hole.

LIE: The position of the ball on the ground. Also the angle of the shaft with the ground when the club is soled correctly.

LINKS: A seaside course.

LIP: The edge, or rim, of the hole or bunker.

L.P.G.A.: Ladies Professional Golf Association.

LOFT OF THE CLUB: The angle of the clubface in relation to the ground.

MAKING THE TURN: The point during a round of golf when a group has just finished the first nine holes and is yet to start the second nine holes.

MASHIE: In the past, the 5-iron was called a mashie.

MATCH PLAY: A competition between two teams or individuals by hole, where the winner is the one with the lowest score on the most holes.

MEDALIST: The player with the lowest score for a qualifying round in a match play tournament.

MEDAL or STROKE PLAY: A competition or tournament where the individual with the lowest number of strokes for a predetermined number of holes is the winner.

MULLIGAN: A common but illegal practice where a player hits a second ball off the first tee because they did not like their first shot, then selects the better of the two shots.

NASSAU: A method of scoring a match, with one point awarded for winning the front nine, one point awarded for winning the back nine and one point awarded for winning the total eighteen.

NECK: The area where the shaft meets the clubhead.

NET SCORE: A player's score after his/her handicap is deducted. For instance, if a player has a score of 90, and subtracts his/her handicap of 15, then the player would have a net score, or adjusted score, of 75.

NIBLICK: In the past, a term used for the 9-iron.

OPEN TOURNAMENT: A tournament where both amateurs and professionals can compete against each other. For instance, The United States Open Championship or The British Open Championship.

OUT-OF-BOUNDS: The area marked with white stakes or a white line where play is prohibited.

OUTSIDE-TO-INSIDE SWING PATH: The opposite of an inside-to-outside swing path, normally resulting in a shot that starts left of the target.

PAR: A standard of scoring excellence based on the length of the hole.

PENALTY STROKE: A stroke or strokes added to your score as outlined in the rules.

PIN HIGH: A shot that lies even with the hole, but to the side, also referred to as hole high.

PITCH SHOT: A short shot hit to the green, with a high trajectory, that rolls very little once it lands on the green.

P.G.A. OF AMERICA: The Professional Golfers' Association of America.

PLAYING THROUGH: A group of players passing a slower group of players with permission.

PLUGGED LIE: When the ball is imbedded in its own impact mark.

POSTURE: The position a golfer puts his/her body in when addressing the ball.

POT BUNKER: A small, deep bunker.

PROVISIONAL BALL: An additional ball hit when a player thinks his/her original ball may be lost or out-of-bounds.

PULLED SHOT: A shot that travels straight, but straight left of the target.

PUNCH SHOT: A low, short shot hit with less than a full-swing.

PUSHED SHOT: A shot that travels straight, but straight right of the target.

ROUGH: The long grass and other vegetation surrounding the fairway and green.

ROYAL AND ANCIENT GOLF CLUB OF ST. ANDREWS, SCOTLAND: The governing body, or association, of the game of golf in Europe.

SAND TRAP: Also known as a bunker.

SAND WEDGE: A club designed with a larger and heavier sole, to make it easier to hit the ball out of the sand. This club may also be used from the grass when near the green.

SCRAMBLE: When you have to show exceptional short game skills to make up for other poor shots on the course. It is common to hear a golfer say that they "had to scramble to get a par." Also, a type of golf event or tournament where each player hits his/her tee shot. The team then selects the best tee shot, and each player hits his/her next shot from that point. This procedure is used until the ball is holed-out.

SCRATCH PLAYER: A highly skilled golfer whose score averages at or below par; and who has a handicap of zero.

SENIORS TOUR: A tour of professional golfers all 50 years of age or more that compete in golf tournaments weekly.

SET UP: The position your body is in when you prepare to make a stroke, also referred to as address.

SHAFT: The long, narrow part of the club that connects the clubhead and the grip.

SHANK: When the ball hits the neck, or hosel, of the club, making the ball go way right or left of the target.

SKYING: Hitting a shot higher and shorter than intended.

SLICE: A shot that curves from left to right.

SLOPE RATING: A number used to compare the difficulty of courses and calculate a player's handicap.

SOLE: The bottom of the club.

SOLE PLATE: A plate, usually metal, located on the bottom of a wood.

SPOON: In the past, the 3-wood was referred to as a spoon.

STANCE: The position of the feet when addressing the golf ball.

SUMMER RULES: When golfers follow the regular rules of the game, which means that you cannot improve the lie of your ball, except for certain circumstances.

SWEET SPOT: The location on the club where you should hit the ball.

SWING ARC: The circle your body and club form when swinging.

SWING PLANE: The angle of the circular motion the club makes in relation to the ground when swinging.

TEE: A small wood or plastic tool used to elevate the ball, which may only be used on the teeing ground.

TEE MARKERS: Markers used to designate the starting point on each hole.

TEEING GROUND: The closely mowed area where the tee markers are set.

TOED SHOT: A shot hit off the toe of the golf club.

TOPPED SHOT: A shot that does not get up into the air because the club hits the top of the ball.

UNDER-CLUBBING: Using a club that will not hit the ball far enough to get to your intended target.

UP: In match play, the number of holes a team or individual is ahead of an opponent,

UP AND DOWN: Holing-out in two strokes when off the green. Allowing one stroke to get the ball onto the green, and one putt to get the ball into the hole.

U.S.G.A.: United States Golf Association, the governing body of golf in the United States.

WAGGLE: Movement of the club or the body just prior to making the golf swing. The waggle helps reduce tension in the golf swing.

WHIFF: A stroke where a golfer swings and misses the golf ball.

WINTER RULES: When a golf course is not in adequate playing condition, therefore allowing golfers to improve the lie of their ball prior to each shot.